BAKING CLASS

50 FUN RECIPES KIDS WILL LOVE TO BAKE!

DEANNA F. COOK

Storey Publishing

The mission of Storey Publishing is to serve our customers by publishing practical information that encourages personal independence in harmony with the environment.

Edited by Deborah Balmuth and Lisa Hiley

Art direction and book design by Jessica Armstrong

Text production by Erin Dawson

Indexed by Nancy D. Wood

Cover and interior photography by © Carl Tremblay, except pages 89 (dough, bottom left), 110 (spoon), 123, and 144 by Mars Vilaubi

Illustrations by © Emily Balsley

The information in this book is true and complete to the best of our knowledge. All recommendations are made without guarantee on the part of the author or Storey Publishing. The author and publisher disclaim any liability in connection with the use of this information.

Storey books are available at special discounts when purchased in bulk for premiums and sales promotions as well as for fundraising or educational use. Special editions or book excerpts can also be created to specification. For details, please call 800-827-8673, or send an email to sales@storey.com.

Storey Publishing
210 MASS MoCA Way
North Adams, MA 01247
storey.com

Printed in China by R.R. Donnelley
10 9 8 7 6

Library of Congress Cataloging-in-Publication Data on file

This book is dedicated to my sweet family.

Acknowledgments

To make this book, I had lots of kitchen helpers. Three cheers and many thanks to the great kids pictured on the pages: Amalia, Amelia, Anna, Caleb, Coco, Dante, Djamil, Eden, Ella, Ethan, Finn, Inez, Luca, Maceo, Maisie, Malia, Ryland, Saenger, Sarah, Sophie, Tate, Tessa, Theo, Zadie H., Zadie S., and Zora.

I also want to thank our photographer, Carl Tremblay, and his assistant, Julian Chappell, for the beautiful photos, and talented food stylist Sally Staub. Special thanks to Jessica Armstrong, Lisa Hiley, and Deborah Balmuth, the team at Storey who helped make this book the best it could be. Thanks, too, to my partners at Kidstir.com for inspiring some of the recipes in this book. Lastly, I couldn't have made this book without the support of my family, who tested and tasted many of the recipes. Thanks Ella, Maisie, and Doug!

To my baking friends: Thanks for picking up *Baking Class*. I hope you enjoy baking up a storm with the recipes in this book. Please share photos of your kitchen creations with me at DeannaFCook.com—I'd love to see what you bake up!

CONTENTS

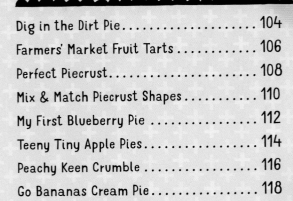

CHAPTER 4
The BREAD BAKERY

CHAPTER 5
The COOKIE JAR

CHAPTER 6
SAVE ROOM for PIE!

CHAPTER 7
CAKE & CUPCAKE FACTORY

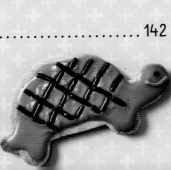

What will you bake?

YAY!

YUMMY TREATS FOR YOU!

BUTTERY ➡️ BISCUITS!, page 50

CHAPTER 1

Welcome to

BAKING CLASS!

Grab your apron and follow these tips and tricks for kitchen fun!

RECIPE RATINGS

Each recipe is rated with one, two, or three rolling pins so you know the skill level needed to complete it. If you are a new chef, you can start with the easier recipes and work your way up.

 **ONE ROLLING PIN**

Most of these recipes are "no-bake" and can be pulled together without having to use the oven.

 **TWO ROLLING PINS**

These recipes involve baking in the oven or toaster oven, so brush up on your oven safety skills before you begin. These are good recipes to work on with a parent or older sibling.

 **THREE ROLLING PINS**

These recipes involve cutting with sharp knives, using an electric mixer or food processor, and using the oven. They tend to take more time to prepare, too.

BAKE LIKE A PRO!

Start good habits from the get-go by following these basic kitchen rules. To begin with, ask an adult for permission before using the kitchen. Ask for help, too, if you have questions along the way.

1. WASH YOUR HANDS with warm water and soap before you handle food.

2. ROLL UP LONG SLEEVES & WEAR AN APRON. TIE BACK LONG HAIR to keep it away from food. You can even wear a bandanna or chef's hat!

3. READ THE RECIPE FROM START TO FINISH before you begin. Follow the steps closely.

4. PUT OUT ALL THE INGREDIENTS you'll need (see the Here's What You Need list) to be sure you have everything.

5. START EACH RECIPE WITH INGREDIENTS THAT ARE AT ROOM TEMPERATURE. And be sure to check expiration dates (don't use baking soda or perishables if they are past their dates).

6. TAKE OUT ALL THE TOOLS you need for your recipe from measuring cups to bowls.

7. MEASURE CAREFULLY (see the tips on page 18).

8. ALWAYS USE POT HOLDERS when moving pans in and out of the oven, and remember to turn the oven off after you're done baking.

9. ARRANGE YOUR OVEN RACKS. Cookies, cakes, and breads bake most evenly in the middle of the oven. So before you preheat, arrange the oven racks so that one is in the center.

10. PREHEAT. Let the oven come to the correct temperature before you put in your pans or cookie trays. Otherwise, your food will take longer to bake or will cook unevenly.

11. LEAVE THE OVEN DOOR SHUT. The temperature drops every time the door is opened, so don't keep opening it to check your food. If your oven has a light, use it to keep an eye on your baked goodies.

12. USE A TIMER. Always set a timer, and don't leave the room when your cookies and pies are baking. Trust your sense of smell. If you smell burning, turn off the oven and take your food out, even if the timer hasn't gone off. Ovens heat at different rates, and no one wants burned baked goods!

13. LEAVE THE KITCHEN SPARKLING CLEAN! Put away the ingredients, wipe down the countertop, and wash the dishes.

GATHER UP THE RIGHT TOOLS

To make the recipes in this book, you'll need some basic baking tools, such as cookie sheets, dry and liquid measuring cups, mixing spoons, and pot holders. You can put together a personal baking kit with your favorite tools and cookie cutters. Just find a big cardboard box or clear plastic container and stock it with your favorite baking tools. Label or decorate your container with the stickers in the back of the book.

This BAKING KIT BELONGS to

RAMEKINS

ROLLING PIN

MIXING BOWLS

CAKE DECORATING KIT (WITH DISPOSABLE PASTRY BAGS AND BASIC ICING TIPS)

PIZZA WHEEL

PASTRY WHEEL

MEASURING SPOONS

APRON

WHISK

PASTRY CUTTER

10

LOAF PANS

COOKIE CUTTERS

DRY MEASURING CUPS

METAL SPATULA

COOKIE SHEET OR SHEET PAN AND PARCHMENT PAPER

MUFFIN PAN

PAPER LINERS

LIQUID MEASURING CUP

PIE DISH

ICING SPATULAS

PASTRY BRUSH

CAKE PANS

RUBBER SPATULA

POT HOLDER

COOLING RACK

Lesson #3

STOCK UP on BAKERY BASICS

Look through the recipes in the book, then make a list of the ingredients you need to make a few of them. If you plan to bake often, it's a good idea to stock up on some of the basics listed below. With the right ingredients in your cupboard, you'll have everything you need to bake up a storm any time you get a craving for cookies!

* FOR GLUTEN-FREE TREATS, SUBSTITUTE GLUTEN-FREE "CUP FOR CUP" FLOUR FOR REGULAR FLOUR IN THE RECIPES.

COCOA POWDER

BUTTER

CINNAMON

POWDERED SUGAR

VEGETABLE OIL

VANILLA EXTRACT

BROWN SUGAR

FLOUR
(WHOLE WHEAT, WHITE, OR GLUTEN-FREE)

WHITE SUGAR

BAKING POWDER
(AND BAKING SODA)

MOLASSES

HONEY

CORNMEAL

SALT

YEAST

OATS

FRESH EGGS

STRAWBERRIES

SHREDDED COCONUT

NUTS

BLUEBERRIES

BANANAS

APPLES

GRATED CARROT

*WHEN FRUITS AND VEGGIES ARE IN SEASON, PICK SOME UP TO ADD TO YOUR BAKED GOODS.

CHOCOLATE CHIPS

CANDY EYES

LEMONS

SUGAR SPRINKLES

COLORED NONPAREILS

RAINBOW SPRINKLES

FOOD COLORING

DRIED FRUIT (RAISINS, DRIED CRANBERRIES)

FUN EXTRAS

BAKING VOCABULARY

Many of the recipes in this book call for some basic prep work, such as melting butter or crushing graham crackers, before you start the other steps. Read the ingredients list and directions all the way through to find out what you need to do before you start baking. Here are some words you'll see in recipes:

STIR. To mix rapidly with a spoon, whisk, spatula, or electric mixer until smooth.

CREAM. To mix butter and sugar together with an electric mixer until it turns fluffy. This adds air to your batter, which helps your baked goods rise.

WHISK. To combine ingredients with a whisk. You can whisk dry ingredients, like flour and baking powder, or wet ingredients, like eggs and milk.

MIX. To use a spoon or electric mixer to combine ingredients evenly. Use a bowl that is big enough to hold everything with extra room for the mixing activity.

PROCESS. To mix ingredients in a food processor. Read the machine manual, and ask an adult for help when using a food processor for the first time. (See Lesson 6: Kitchen Safety, page 19.)

GREASE THE PAN. To rub butter or vegetable oil (or use baking spray) on baking pans so food won't stick. Don't forget the sides and corners of the pan!

GREASE AND LIGHTLY FLOUR. Once you've greased your pan, add a tablespoon of flour. Tap all sides to lightly flour the entire surface.

LINE WITH PARCHMENT. To lay a sheet of parchment paper on your pan, which will keep cookies and breads from sticking to them.

KNEAD. To fold the dough in half, press with your palms, then turn and fold again. This makes your scones and breads light and airy by developing the gluten.

MELT. To turn a solid into a liquid by applying heat. You can melt butter or chocolate in a saucepan over low heat or in a bowl in a microwave for 10 to 20 seconds at a time.

BRUSH. To paint melted butter or egg wash on dough or bread with a pastry brush.

Lesson continues on next page.

SIFT. To process flour and other dry ingredients through a sieve or sifter to break up any clumps. Most flour you buy in the store is presifted, but if your baking powder or baking soda looks lumpy, you might want to sift it with the flour to mix it all together.

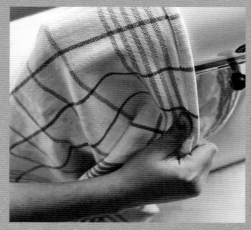

ADD DRY INGREDIENTS. To add a mixture of flour and other dry ingredients to a batter. If you're using a stand mixer, you can prevent the flour from flying around the kitchen by carefully holding a dishtowel around the bowl, keeping fingers out of the way.

CUT IN THE BUTTER. To use a special pastry cutter, or two forks, to combine butter or shortening with dry ingredients until crumbly.

ROLL OUT. To flatten out dough with a rolling pin. Rolling between two pieces of plastic wrap or waxed paper prevents sticking. You won't need to add extra flour, which can make your baked goods taste less buttery.

CUT WITH COOKIE CUTTERS. To cut into shapes using cookie cutters. Use the sharper side to press into the dough. Cold dough is easiest to cut. If it sticks to the cutters, dip them in a little flour.

CUT WITH A WHEEL. To cut dough or piecrust with a pastry wheel or a pizza wheel. The pastry wheel makes a zigzag pattern. The pizza wheel makes a straight line.

CRIMP. To pinch the edges of a dough into a decorative pattern, or to press two edges of dough together to seal them.

GRATE. To shred ingredients, such as carrots or zucchini, against a grater. When the food you're grating gets really small, stop grating to protect your fingers. Grating citrus rind is called zesting. (Note: you can also use a cool tool called a zester to grate the rind.)

SCOOP. To make drop cookies or fill muffin pans using an ice cream scoop. It's less messy than using a spoon, and the cookies, muffins, and cupcakes will come out evenly shaped.

SCRAPE WITH A SPATULA. To get every last bit of batter out of the mixing bowl with a rubber spatula.

TEST FOR DONENESS. To check to see if your baked goods are finished baking.

COOL. To let your baked goods cool down after baking. Some baked goods you can eat right away, but others need to cool in the pan or on a rack. Follow the recipe instructions.

Equivalents & Conversions

Here's a handy chart to help you convert recipe measurements.

1 TEASPOON
= 5 milliliters

1 TABLESPOON
= 3 teaspoons
(or ½ fluid ounce)
= 15 milliliters

¼ CUP
= 4 tablespoons
= 60 milliliters

½ CUP
= 4 ounces
= 120 milliliters

1 CUP
= 8 ounces
= 240 milliliters

1 PINT
= 2 cups
= 16 ounces
= 475 milliliters

1 QUART
= 2 pints
= 0.95 liters

Lesson #5

MEASURE CAREFULLY

When following a recipe, it's important to measure the ingredients carefully. Here are some tips.

LIQUID INGREDIENTS. Measure larger amounts of milk, water, and other liquids in a glass or plastic liquid measuring cup. Pour the liquid into the cup and read the measure from eye level.

For smaller measures, like a teaspoon, use measuring spoons. Work over a small bowl to catch any spills.

DRY INGREDIENTS. It's important to measure flour, sugar, and other dry ingredients with dry measuring cups or measuring spoons that can be leveled off. Fill the cup or spoon with the ingredient, and then run the flat part of a butter knife across it to get an exact measure.

BUTTER. Follow the measurement marks on the butter package. Find the line for the correct measurement, and then carefully cut straight down on the stick through the paper. Unwrap the portion you need and add it to your recipe.

Lesson #6
KITCHEN SAFETY

Many of the recipes in this book require that you keep safety measures in mind, especially when you use sharp knives, an electric mixer, or a hot oven. It's important to work safely in the kitchen, so here are some tips.

KNIVES & GRATERS.

Make sure your knife is sharpened properly (dull knives are more dangerous because they can slip while you're cutting), and hold it firmly, with your fingers out of the way of the blade. Always cut with the blade moving away from your hand.

When you use a grater, watch out that you don't accidentally scrape the tip of your finger or your knuckles. That can hurt a lot! Dry your hands when cutting and grating — wet hands are slippery!

MIXERS AND FOOD PROCESSORS. Keep

your fingers out of the way of the beaters when working with an electric mixer.

With a food processor, be especially careful when you are fitting the blades into the machine or taking them out to be washed. Never try to operate a food processor with the lid off, and of course, never stick a spoon or spatula into the bowl without turning the machine completely off first.

MICROWAVE.

Different microwave ovens have different directions, so ask an adult to show you how to use yours. Never use metal or aluminum foil in the microwave. Always use microwave-safe dishes. Glass, paper towels, and some plastic containers are fine. The wrong material could damage the microwave or even cause a fire.

OVEN, STOVETOP, AND TOASTER OVEN. Before you

turn on the stove or oven, check first with an adult. He or she can show you the proper way to use the range and explain the different settings. When you are cooking something on the stove, always stay in the kitchen!

- Always use oven mitts when handling hot pans and baking trays.

- When you open the oven, avoid the blast of heat that will rise up in your face.

- Turn pan handles to the side so the pans don't accidentally get knocked off the stove.

- Switch off the stovetop or oven when you have finished cooking.

SERVE UP SOME SPECIAL TREATS

When your fresh-baked goods are ready to serve, your friends and family will be happy to enjoy them. Here are some ways to make the most of your treats.

EAT THEM FRESH. Most of the foods made from recipes in this book taste best the day they're made. But a few, like Monkey Munch Banana Bread (page 58) and Zombie Zucchini Bread (page 60), actually taste better a day later. Check the recipe for serving and storage suggestions.

PACK 'EM UP. Store your baked goods in sealable containers or plastic bags. Most of the items can be stored at room temperature and will last a few days. You can also store unbaked piecrust and cookie, cracker, and bread dough in the freezer for up to 1 month.

Made for You by: Djamil

GIVE A KITCHEN GIFT. Baked treats make great gifts for teachers, friends, and family members. Bring your parents and siblings a basket of breakfast breads in bed on their birthdays or special days. Wrap up cookies or homemade breads for teachers and friends. Use the fun labels and gift tags at the back of the book to make your goodies special.

CELEBRATE WITH SWEETS! Mark a big birthday or holiday with a special homemade cake or decorated cupcakes. See Bake Up a Birthday Party (page 127) and Mix & Match Cupcake Decorating Party (page 134) for some ideas. Make any celebration more fun with the stickers in the back of the book.

MAKE SPECIAL HOLIDAY TREATS. Bake up some holiday fun throughout the year. Make cookie hearts for Valentine's Day or reindeer for Christmas (page 91), Pumpkin Patch Muffins for Halloween (page 30), and cookies decorated like turkeys for Thanksgiving (page 90).

MUFFINS
$1 each

Gingersnaps
a... 1.00

I Love Chocolate

scones
$1.00

Host a Bake Sale!

Looking to raise money for your school or a charity? Host a bake sale. Follow these tips for successful sales. Check the fun extras at the back of the book to make your sale special.

SET UP THE SALE. Cover your table with a tablecloth. Include a vase of flowers or other seasonal decoration.

PRICE IT RIGHT. Include a sign with all the prices.

MAKE THE FOOD LOOK YUMMY! Serve most of the cookies and bars in individually wrapped containers with handmade wrappers and stickers. You can decorate using the stickers and labels at the back of the book.

INCLUDE A RECIPE CARD. You can write down the recipe and give it away.

ADVERTISE! Create a fun sign to post to spread the word.

RISE and SHINE

BAKE UP
a Morning
Surprise!

BURSTING
WITH
BLUEBERRIES
MUFFINS,
page 32

CHAPTER 2

Good Morning
TREATS

Wake up to some toasty baked goodies for breakfast!

A TOAST TO YOU!

Makes 1 serving

Here's a simple trick for making personalized toast. All you need is a piece of bread and a piece of foil. When your toast is ready, spread on a little butter and serve it up for a fun breakfast!

Here's What You Need

1 piece of bread
  Aluminum foil
  Toaster oven

HERE'S WHAT YOU DO

1.

Roll a piece of foil into a letter or shape a little smaller than the piece of bread. Try the first initial of your name or a heart.

2.

Place the letter on the bread. Turn your toaster oven on to the "toast" setting. Place the bread on the toaster rack, and toast until brown.

3.

Remove the toast and the foil, and voilà!

SPREAD THE LOVE!

Jazz up your homemade toasts, muffins, and breads with flavored butter or cream cheese. Start with 2 tablespoons softened cream cheese or butter and add 1 to 2 teaspoons of the fillings listed here. Stir 'em up and spread 'em on thick!

RASPBERRY JAM

Orange Marmalade

Pumpkin Pie Spice

SUN-DRIED TOMATOES

SWEET HONEY

GRAPE JELLY

Fresh Herbs + Garlic

MIX & MATCH
TOAST TOPPERS

Check out these cool ideas for jazzing up your breakfast plate. Gather the ingredients you need, then toast up a slice of bread, English muffin, or bagel and have some fun making these or creating your own.

SMART OWL
Toast + Almond Butter + Fruit Face + Kiwi Wings

WHOOO WHOOO

EGGS IN A NEST
Bread + Cookie Cutter Hole + Fried Egg

BREAKFAST PIZZA
Bagel + Tomato Sauce + Mozzarella Cheese

HEALTHY HUMMUS
Whole-Grain Toast + Hummus + Edamame + Salt & Pepper

S'MORE TOAST

Chocolate-Hazelnut Spread + Toasted Mini Marshmallows

KITTY

Bagel + Strawberry Ears and Mouth + Banana Whiskers + Blueberry Eyes + Raisin Nose

CINNAMON TOAST

Toast + Butter + Cinnamon Sugar

FRUIT FLOWERS

Bagel + Cream Cheese + Berry and Orange Petals + Kiwi Center

SMASHED AVOCADO TOAST

Toast + Avocado Slices + Salt & Pepper

TOASTER-OVEN TARTS

Makes 6–8

For a special treat, make your own boxed breakfast tarts from scratch with this fun and easy recipe.

Here's What You Need

- 2 unbaked piecrusts (see page 108)
- 1 small jar strawberry or raspberry jam
- 1 cup confectioners' sugar
- 2 tablespoons milk
  Rainbow sprinkles

Preheat the oven to 425°F (220°C).

HERE'S WHAT YOU DO

1.

Roll out the piecrusts to ¼ inch thick. Cut each piecrust into 6 to 8 rectangles, about 5 by 3 inches each. (You can use a ruler.)

2.

Place half of the rectangles on a cookie sheet lined with parchment paper.

3.

Spread 1 to 2 teaspoons of jam in the center of each rectangle, leaving the edges plain. Top with another rectangle.

4.

Crimp around all four edges of each tart with a fork.

5.

Bake for 7 to 10 minutes, or until just brown. Cool on the cookie sheet for a minute or two, then transfer them to a cooling rack.

6.

Mix up a glaze for your tarts by combining the confectioners' sugar with the milk, mixing in 1 tablespoon of milk at a time.

7.

Stir it up until it's nice and smooth.

8.

When the tarts are cool, spread some glaze over each one with a butter knife.

9.

Decorate with sprinkles.

TIP: Store toaster tarts in an airtight container. To warm them up, heat flat in a toaster oven. (Don't toast them in a regular toaster — they'll collapse!)

Pumpkins Galore

PUMPKIN CHOCOLATE CHIP MUFFINS: Stir ½ cup chocolate chips into the batter before scooping it into the muffin pan.

PUMPKIN DRIED FRUIT MUFFINS: Stir ½ cup raisins or dried cranberries into the batter before scooping it into the muffin pan.

PUMPKIN PATCH MUFFINS

Makes 12

Serve up a basket of these moist, wholesome muffins for a fall treat or a spooky Halloween breakfast.

Here's What You Need

2 cups flour (or 1 cup white and 1 cup whole-wheat flour)	½ teaspoon baking powder	2 eggs
1 tablespoon cinnamon	½ teaspoon salt	1¼ cups sugar
1 teaspoon baking soda	½ teaspoon allspice (or ground cloves)	1 cup pumpkin pureé (canned or fresh)
	¼ teaspoon nutmeg	½ cup vegetable oil
		½ cup milk or water

Preheat the oven to 375°F (190°C).

1. Stir the flour, cinnamon, baking soda, baking powder, salt, allspice, and nutmeg in a medium bowl.

2. Whisk the eggs in a large bowl.

3. Add the sugar, pumpkin, vegetable oil, and milk to the eggs. Mix well.

4. Add the pumpkin mixture to the dry ingredients.

5. Stir until all the flour is mixed in.

6. Line a 12-cup muffin pan with paper liners or grease the cups. Spoon or scoop the batter into the muffin cups, filling them about two-thirds full.

Bake the muffins for 20 minutes, or until a toothpick inserted into the center comes out clean.

Bursting with BLUEBERRIES MUFFINS

Makes 12

Packed with fresh blueberries, these sweet muffins are a nice morning surprise.

Preheat the oven to 375°F (190°C).

Here's What You Need

- 2 cups flour (or 1 cup white and 1 cup whole-wheat flour)
- 2 teaspoons baking powder
- ½ teaspoon baking soda
- ¼ teaspoon salt
- ½ cup (1 stick) butter, softened
- 1 cup sugar
- 2 eggs
- 1 teaspoon vanilla extract
- ½ cup milk
- 2 cups blueberries

HERE'S WHAT YOU DO

1.
Stir the flour, baking powder, baking soda, and salt in a medium bowl.

2.
Cream the butter and sugar in a separate large bowl with an electric mixer until fluffy. Beat in the eggs, one at a time. Stir in the vanilla.

3.
Blend in half the flour mixture, and then half the milk.

4.

Add the rest of the flour and milk, and blend.

5.

Add the blueberries to the batter, and use a rubber spatula to fold them in.

6.

Line a 12-cup muffin pan with paper liners or grease the cups. Fill the muffin cups almost to the top with the batter.

7.

Bake for 25 minutes, or until light brown.

Streusel Topping!

Add a little extra flavor and crunch to your blueberry muffins with a tasty topping.

In a bowl, mix up:

6 tablespoons flour

2½ tablespoons melted butter

1 tablespoon sugar

1 tablespoon brown sugar

⅛ teaspoon cinnamon

¼ teaspoon vanilla extract

You can do this with a fork or your clean hands. Sprinkle the streusel on top of the muffins before baking.

CARROT APPLESAUCE BITES

Makes 24 mini muffins

These applesauce muffins are easy to mix up by hand. You can add a secret healthy ingredient for extra flavor and nutrition: grated carrot. For a simpler muffin, skip the carrots.

Preheat the oven to 350°F (180°C).

Here's What You Need

- 1½ cups whole-wheat flour
- 1½ teaspoons cinnamon
- 1 teaspoon baking powder
- ½ teaspoon baking soda
- ½ teaspoon salt
- 2 eggs
- ⅔ cup brown sugar
- 4 tablespoons butter, melted
- 1 cup unsweetened applesauce
- ½ cup grated carrot

1.

Line two 12-cup mini muffin pans with paper liners or grease the cups.

2.

Stir the flour, cinnamon, baking powder, baking soda, and salt in a medium bowl.

3.

Whisk the eggs in a separate bowl. Mix in the brown sugar. Then add the melted butter and applesauce. Stir in the grated carrot.

4.

Pour the applesauce mixture over the flour mixture, and stir until all the flour is mixed in.

5.

Spoon the batter into the muffin cups, filling each one about two-thirds full.

6.

Bake the muffins for 15 to 20 minutes, or until light brown.

Fancy FRENCH BREAKFAST TREATS

Makes 12

It's fun (and tasty!) to dip the warm muffins into melted butter and roll them up in cinnamon sugar.

Here's What You Need

MUFFINS
- 2 cups flour
- ¾ cup sugar
- 2 teaspoons baking powder
- ½ teaspoon salt
- ¼ teaspoon nutmeg
- 1 egg
- 1¼ cups milk
- 6 tablespoons butter, melted
- 1 teaspoon vanilla extract

TOPPING
- ⅔ cup sugar
- 1 teaspoon cinnamon
- 3 tablespoons butter, melted

Preheat the oven to 350°F (180°C).

1. Stir the flour, sugar, baking powder, salt, and nutmeg in a large bowl.

2. In a separate bowl, whisk the egg. Mix in the milk, melted butter, and vanilla.

3. Pour the egg mixture over the flour mixture, and stir until all the flour is mixed in.

4. Line a 12-cup muffin pan with paper liners or grease the cups. Spoon the batter into the muffin cups, filling each about two-thirds full. Bake the muffins for 20 minutes, or until light brown.

5. While the muffins cool slightly, mix the sugar and cinnamon in a small bowl. Pour the melted butter into a separate bowl.

6. Roll the warm muffins first in the melted butter and then in the cinnamon sugar.

CRANBERRY ORANGE SCONES

Makes 8

Start your day with a fruity Scottish scone. Serve them up warm with a little butter and a cup of fruit tea!

Here's What You Need

- 2 cups flour
- 3 tablespoons sugar
- 2 teaspoons baking powder
- ½ teaspoon salt
- ½ cup (1 stick) cold butter, cut into chunks
- 1 egg
- ½ cup milk
- ¼ cup dried cranberries
- 1 teaspoon grated orange zest

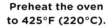

Preheat the oven to 425°F (220°C).

HERE'S WHAT YOU DO

1.

Mix the flour, sugar, baking powder, and salt in a large bowl.

2.

Use a pastry cutter or fork to cut the butter into the dough until it looks crumbly.

3.

Whisk the egg and milk in a separate bowl. Pour the egg mixture over the flour mixture. Add the cranberries and orange zest, and stir it up.

4.

Dust your hands and a cutting board with flour. Knead the dough for a few minutes, and then pat it into a 7-inch circle.

5.

Place the dough onto an ungreased cookie sheet. Cut it into 8 wedges with a pizza wheel or knife.

6.

Separate the triangles so they are at least an inch apart. Bake for 15 to 18 minutes, or until golden.

Scones are best served warm!

KITCHEN CREATIVITY

Scone Stir-Ins

Skip the cranberries and orange zest, and try one of these combos instead or make up your own!

CURRANT SCONES: Mix in ¼ cup dried currants or raisins.

CHOCOLATE CHERRY: Add ¼ cup chocolate chips and 2 tablespoons chopped dried cherries.

LEMON GINGER: Add ¼ cup diced candied ginger and 2 teaspoons grated lemon zest.

CHEDDAR ROSEMARY: Skip the sugar, and add ⅓ cup grated cheddar and 1 teaspoon finely chopped rosemary.

Scones

AWESOME!!

CURE YOUR SNACK ATTACK!

YUM!

PUFFY ⇨ POPOVERS, page 46

CHAPTER 3

CRACKERS & QUICK BREADS

Cure a snack attack with these homemade munchies!

CRUNCHY TORTILLA CHIPS
& Nachos

Makes 4 servings

Craving a crunchy snack? Bake up a quick batch of tortilla chips in the oven, then turn them into nachos!

Here's What You Need

6   spinach, flour, whole-wheat, or corn tortillas

1–2   tablespoons olive oil
      Salt

30   tortilla chips

FOR NACHOS

¼   cup salsa

½   cup grated Monterey Jack cheese

Preheat the oven to 350°F (180°C).

1.

Cut each tortilla into triangles with a pizza cutter or kitchen scissors. Or cut the tortillas into shapes with cookie cutters.

2.

Spread the tortilla pieces on an ungreased baking sheet in a single layer. Use a pastry brush to coat both sides of the tortillas with oil.

3.

Bake the chips for 8 to 10 minutes, turning them over halfway, until lightly browned on both sides. Sprinkle with salt and serve, or . . .

4.

Leave the chips on the baking sheet when they come out of the oven and spoon on a little salsa.

5.

Sprinkle the chips with grated cheese.

6.

Bake for about 5 minutes, or until the cheese melts. Serve with extra salsa for dipping!

HOW TO MINCE GARLIC CLOVES

Ever tried using a garlic press? It's fun and easy to use. First pull off a clove from a head of garlic. Remove the papery skin. Place the clove in the press, and then squeeze the handles together to mince the garlic.

QUICK CROUTONS

Makes 2 cups

Add some crunch to an ordinary salad with this tasty toasted topping. You can bake them in an oven or a toaster oven!

Here's What You Need

3–4 slices whole-wheat, sourdough, or other bread
3 tablespoons olive oil
1 clove garlic, minced
½ teaspoon salt
1 teaspoon dried basil, optional
½ teaspoon dried oregano, optional

Preheat the oven to 375°F (190°C).

1.

Cut the bread into cubes with a serrated knife. Arrange the cubes in a single layer on a baking sheet or toaster oven tray. (Line the baking sheet with aluminum foil for easier cleanup.)

2.

Mix the olive oil, garlic, and salt in a small bowl. For a little extra flavor, add the dried basil and oregano.

3.

Paint the olive oil mixture evenly over the bread cubes with a pastry brush.

4.

Bake the croutons for 6 to 10 minutes, or until light brown.

PUFFY POPOVERS

Makes 12

These treats are light and airy and yummy! Bake up a batch as a quick and easy after-school snack.

Preheat the oven to 375°F (190°C).

Here's What You Need

1–2	tablespoons butter
2	eggs
1	cup milk
1	cup flour
½	teaspoon salt

HERE'S WHAT YOU DO

1. Place a small pat of butter in the center of each cup in a 12-cup muffin pan. Put the pan in the oven for just a minute or two to melt the butter, and then take it out.

2. Whisk the eggs in a large bowl. Add the milk, flour, and salt. Whisk until most of the lumps are gone.

3. Transfer the batter to a large measuring cup for easy pouring. Pour the batter into the buttered muffin pan cups, filling each about two-thirds full.

4. Bake the popovers for 30 to 35 minutes, or until golden brown and puffy. Remove the pan from the oven. Carefully pop them out of the muffin pan with a butter knife. Eat right away! They're extra delicious with jam and honey.

A SCIENCE EXPERIMENT YOU CAN EAT!

Did you know that all baking is basically kitchen chemistry? Baking combines various ingredients and uses heat (and sometimes other steps, like kneading dough) to create a reaction that turns the ingredients into something different.

To make a perfect popover that's crispy on the outside and hollow on the inside, you need a hot oven, flour, and eggs. Imagine your popover is like a hot air balloon: The shell of the balloon is made of the protein in the eggs and flour. The steam comes from the hot liquid (the milk) heating up and evaporating. As it fills with hot air, the balloon "pops over" the sides of the pan, making it a tasty chemistry experiment!

CRISPY CHEESE SQUARES

Makes about 2 dozen

If you're a fan of cheese-flavored crackers, try making them from scratch with real shredded cheese. You may never eat them from a box again!

Preheat the oven to 350°F (180°C).

Here's What You Need

- 2 cups (8 ounces) shredded cheddar cheese
- 4 tablespoons butter, cut into chunks
- 1 cup flour
- ¼ teaspoon salt
- 3 tablespoons milk

Special Equipment

Food processor

HERE'S WHAT YOU DO

1.

Combine the cheese, butter chunks, flour, and salt in the bowl of a food processor. Pulse until the mixture looks crumbly.

2.

Pour the milk through the top of the food processor. Mix until the dough starts to stick together.

3.

Remove the dough from the bowl, gathering the crumbs together into two balls.

4.

Flatten the balls into disks between sheets of plastic wrap. Wrap them up, and refrigerate for at least 10 minutes (or up to 3 days).

5.

Roll the dough to ¼-inch thickness. (If it's too hard to roll, let it soften on the counter for a few minutes.)

6.

Cut the dough into 1-inch squares with a knife or a pastry or pizza cutter (or cut it into shapes with a small cookie cutter).

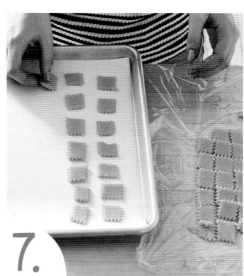

7.

Place the crackers on a baking sheet lined with parchment paper.

8.

Wiggle a toothpick in the center of each square to make a hole. Bake for 8 to 12 minutes, or until crispy. Cool on the pan for a few minutes before eating them.

BUTTERY BISCUITS!

Makes 10–12

Biscuit dough is a little like Play-Doh. You can shape it, roll it, and cut it up into stars and hearts. Here's a favorite recipe from the book *Cooking Class*.

Here's What You Need

2 cups flour
1 tablespoon baking powder
1 tablespoon sugar
1 teaspoon salt
5 tablespoons cold butter
¾ cup milk

Preheat the oven to 425°F (220°C).

1. Whisk the flour, baking powder, sugar, and salt in a large bowl. Cut the butter into small chunks. Use a pastry cutter or fork to mix the butter into the dry ingredients until the dough is crumbly.

2. Pour in the milk. Stir until it forms a rough ball. You can switch to mixing with your (clean!) hands if it's too hard to stir. The dough will be a little bit sticky, so dip your hands in flour first.

3. Transfer the dough to a countertop dusted with flour. Knead the dough a few times, then shape it into a large ball.

4. Pat the dough into a flat circle about ½ inch thick (the biscuits will double in thickness as they bake).

5. Dip a cookie cutter in flour and use it to cut out the biscuits. Place them a few inches apart on an ungreased or parchment-lined baking sheet. Bake the biscuits for 12 minutes, or until lightly browned.

SILLY STICKS

Makes 12

Puff pastry is a buttery dough that bakes up into lots of crispy layers. It's pretty tricky to make from scratch, but the store-bought kind tastes almost as good as homemade. And within minutes, you can bake up a variety of snacks and treats like these cheesy sticks.

Here's What You Need

- 1 sheet (½ box) frozen puff pastry, thawed for 40 minutes
- 1 egg
- ½ cup shredded Parmesan or cheddar cheese
- 1 teaspoon Italian herbs, poppy seeds, or sesame seeds
- ½ teaspoon salt
  A pinch of black pepper

Preheat the oven to 375°F (190°C).

375°

HERE'S WHAT YOU DO

1.

Lightly flour a counter or cutting board. Use a rolling pin to roll out the puff pastry into a rectangle around 10 by 12 inches.

2.

Whisk the egg with 1 tablespoon of water. Brush it all over the pastry. Sprinkle the cheese, herbs, salt, and pepper over the pastry. Lightly press the cheese into the puff pastry.

Playing with PUFF PASTRY

A box of puff pastry has two sheets, and you only need one for the Silly Straws. Here are some fun ideas for using the other sheet. Depending on the shape, bake at 375°F (190°C) for 12 to 25 minutes, or until light brown and puffed up. Bake on a cookie sheet lined with parchment paper, and keep an eye on your creations to make sure they don't burn.

- **CINNAMON TWISTS.** Cut into strips, sprinkle with cinnamon sugar, twist, and bake.

- **SWEET STRAWBERRY BITES.** Line a mini muffin pan with small squares of pastry, and bake. Fill the crispy cups with pudding, and top with sliced strawberries.

- **RUSTIC PIE.** Choose your favorite fruit topping — see page 106 for directions.

- **FLATBREAD PIZZA.** Roll out the pastry, top with pasta sauce and cheese and veggies, and bake.

- **TURNOVERS.** Cut the pastry into 3-inch squares, fill each one with jam or chopped fresh fruit, fold into a triangular pocket, and bake.

3.

Cut each sheet the long way with a pizza wheel into a dozen strips.

4.

Twist each strip, and lay on a baking sheet lined with parchment paper. Bake for 12 to 15 minutes, or until light brown and puffed up.

CRACKIN' CORN BREAD

Makes 6–8 servings

Cornmeal, which is ground-up dried corn, makes a hearty quick bread. Serve it with a big bowl of chili.

Here's What You Need

- 1 cup cornmeal
- 1 cup flour
- 3 tablespoons sugar
- 2 teaspoons baking powder
- ¼ teaspoon salt
- 2 eggs
- 1 cup milk
- ¼ cup vegetable oil or melted butter

Preheat the oven to 425°F (220°C).

HERE'S WHAT YOU DO

1. Stir together the cornmeal, flour, sugar, baking powder, and salt in a large bowl.

2. In a separate bowl, whisk the eggs, milk, and oil.

3.

Pour the egg mixture over the cornmeal mixture. Stir it all up.

4.

Grease an 8-inch baking dish and pour the batter in.

5.

Tilt the pan to spread the batter evenly. Tap it lightly on the countertop to remove air bubbles.

6.

Bake for 20 minutes, or until the edges begin to brown. You'll know it's done when a toothpick inserted in the center comes out clean. Cool slightly before cutting and serving.

KITCHEN CREATIVITY

Southern Corn Sticks!

For corn bread that looks like fresh ears of corn from the garden, try this trick. Place two 7-stick cast-iron corn molds in the oven. Turn the heat to 425°F (220°C) and warm up the pans for 15 minutes. Have a grown-up help you carefully remove the hot pans from the oven. Brush the molds with melted butter.

Fill the corn sticks almost to the top with batter. Place the pan back into the oven, and bake 10 to 12 minutes, or until a toothpick inserted in the middle comes out clean. While they are still warm, pop them out of the pan and enjoy.

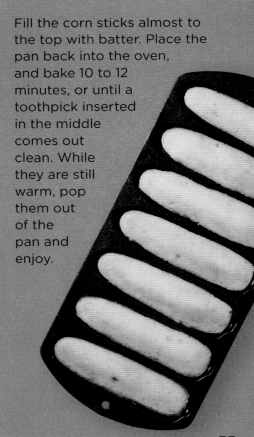

UNDER THE SEA WORLD

READY TO DIVE INTO A FUN COOKING ART PROJECT? Check out these cool ideas for turning ordinary food into an underwater world. Crush some graham crackers into crumbs for the sand and get creative with crackers (crabs, sea turtles, and castles), tortillas (sea weed and snorkelers), cheese (coral, fins, sails, octopus), and pretzel sticks (fishing poles, crab legs, and more). Admire and then enjoy your edible creation, from sea to shining sea!

Monkey Munch
BANANA
BREAD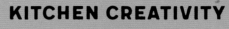

Makes 2 loaves

Got a pile of overripe bananas sitting on your countertop? Don't toss them out. Use them to make banana bread. The riper the banana, the sweeter the bread!

Here's What You Need

- 4 overripe bananas
- ½ cup vegetable oil
- 1¼ cups sugar
- 2 eggs
- 2 cups flour
- 2 teaspoons baking soda
- 1 teaspoon salt
- 1 tablespoon wheat germ, optional

Preheat the oven to 350°F (180°C).

KITCHEN CREATIVITY
Monkey Bread!

Go bananas for this silly snack. Spread a slice of banana bread with peanut butter or chocolate-hazelnut spread. Top with banana ears and a mouth and blueberry eyes.

1.

Mash the bananas in a bowl with a fork. Set aside.

2.

Blend the vegetable oil and sugar with an electric mixer in a large bowl.

3.

Add the eggs and mashed bananas, and blend well.

4.

In a separate bowl, stir together the flour, baking soda, salt, and wheat germ, if using.

5.

Add the dry ingredients to the banana mixture and stir it up.

6.

Grease two loaf pans and divide the batter evenly between them. Bake for 50 to 60 minutes. The bread is done when the top springs back after you gently press it in the center.

ZOMBIE ZUCCHINI BREAD 🍞🍞🍞

Makes 1 loaf

If you have too many zucchinis in your garden, don't toss them in the compost heap (where they'll turn into zombies!). Grate one up, and mix it into this tasty quick bread.

Here's What You Need

- 1 small zucchini
- 1½ cups flour
- 1½ teaspoons cinnamon
- 1 teaspoon baking powder
- ½ teaspoon baking soda
- ½ teaspoon salt
- 2 eggs
- 1 cup sugar
- ½ cup vegetable oil
- 1½ teaspoons vanilla extract

Preheat the oven to 350°F (180°C).

KITCHEN CREATIVITY
Make 'Em Mini

For a quick gift from the kitchen, bake your zucchini bread batter in mini loaf or fun-shaped pans. Grease the pans, and fill halfway with batter. Then bake at 350°F (180°C) for 35 minutes. For an extra cute gift, leave the loaf in the pan. Add a tag from the back of the book!

1.

Carefully grate the zucchini, keeping fingers tucked away from the blade. Measure out 1¼ cups, and set aside.

2.

Stir together the flour, cinnamon, baking powder, baking soda, and salt in a large mixing bowl.

3.

Whisk the eggs in a separate bowl.

4.

Mix the sugar into the eggs, and then add the oil, vanilla, and grated zucchini.

5.

Pour the zucchini mixture over the flour mixture, and stir it up.

6.

Grease a loaf pan and scrape the batter into it. Bake for 50 to 60 minutes, or until a toothpick inserted in the middle comes out clean.

Fresh Baked
BREAD

Mmmmmmmm...

EASY-PEASY
BREAD DOUGH,
page 66

CHAPTER 4

The BREAD BAKERY

It's not hard to make yummy yeast breads from scratch — here's how!

* GARLIC BREAD STICKS, 64

* MIX & MATCH BREAD ART, 74

* EASY-PEASY BREAD DOUGH, 66

* SIMPLE SANDWICH LOAF, 68

* BRAID AWAY BREAD, 70

* SWEET CINNAMON, ROLLS, 72

* NO NEED TO KNEAD BREAD, 76

* IT'S A PARTY! PIZZA DOUGH, 78

GARLIC BREAD STICKS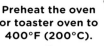

Makes 4–6 servings

On spaghetti night, serve up these garlicky bread sticks and watch them disappear fast!

Here's What You Need

- 1 baguette
- 4 tablespoons butter
- 2 garlic cloves, minced
- ¼ cup shredded Parmesan cheese, optional

Preheat the oven or toaster oven to 400°F (200°C).

HERE'S WHAT YOU DO

1. Carefully cut a baguette in half the long way, and then cut each half into 1-inch slices. Ask a grown-up for help if you need it.

2. Place the butter in a small bowl and melt it in a microwave. Add the crushed garlic clove and stir. Brush each slice of bread with the garlic butter, and then place it butter side up on an ungreased baking sheet.

3. For cheesy garlic bread, sprinkle with the Parmesan.

Bake for 2 to 5 minutes, or until lightly toasted. Watch very closely so it doesn't burn!

Fun with FRENCH BREAD

Turn a loaf of French bread from your local bakery into fun food!

SILLY SLIPPERS

Cut off the ends of small baguettes to make slippers as shown. Serve at a sleepover party for breakfast!

SLITHERING SNAKE

Make your favorite sandwich on a loaf of French bread. Then cut it into 2-inch slices. Arrange the mini sandwiches on a platter in a snake shape. Add olive eyes and a green pepper tongue to the snake's face.

PULL-APART PIZZA

Arrange slices of French bread into a pizza shape on a cookie sheet. Top with pizza sauce, pepperoni slices, and shredded mozzarella. Bake for 15 minutes at 350°F (180°C), or until the cheese is nice and bubbly.

Easy-Peasy BREAD DOUGH

Makes 2 loaves

Craving a slice of fresh bread? This basic recipe bakes up two delicious loaves that you can use to make toast for breakfast and sandwiches for lunch. Or check out the variations on the following pages, and make a braided loaf, cinnamon rolls, or bread art. Each of the variations calls for using half of the dough made here, so you can try at least two with one batch of dough.

Here's What You Need

- 1 tablespoon (1 packet) active dry yeast
- 2 tablespoons sugar
- 2 cups warm water (it should feel like bathwater)
- 1 tablespoon salt
- 6 cups white or whole-wheat flour, or a combo
- 1 tablespoon olive oil

HERE'S WHAT YOU DO

1.

To make any kind of yeast bread, you need to "proof" the yeast, to make sure it's active so the dough will rise. To do this, add the yeast and sugar to the warm water, and whisk until dissolved.

2.

Let it sit for about 5 minutes, or until tiny bubbles appear on the surface. Whisk in the salt, and then add the flour, 1 cup at a time, mixing after each addition.

3.

Switch to mixing with your (clean!) hands until you can form the dough into a sticky ball.

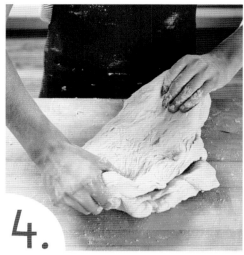

4.

Dust your hands and countertop with flour. Place the dough on the counter, and knead until it is smooth and elastic. (See the kneading tips at right.) This can take up to 10 minutes.

5.

Grease a clean bowl with the olive oil. Place the dough in the bowl and turn to coat with oil. Cover the bowl with plastic wrap. Let the dough rise at room temperature for 1 to 2 hours, or until doubled in size.

6.

Punch the dough down (this is the fun part!). Knead it again for just a few minutes to remove air bubbles. Now your dough is ready to shape into any of the loaves on pages 68 to 75.

HOW TO KNEAD

1 Push the dough down and away from you with the heels of your hands.

2 Fold the dough in half.

3 Rotate the dough a quarter turn and repeat steps 1, 2, and 3 until the dough is smooth and stretchy. This can take up to 10 minutes, so be patient!

Simple SANDWICH LOAF

Makes 1 or 2 loaves

Here's What You Need

Easy-Peasy Bread Dough, page 66 (use the full amount for two loaves or half for one loaf)

Preheat the oven to 375°F (190°C).

1.

If you're making two loaves from a full batch of dough, cut the dough in half.

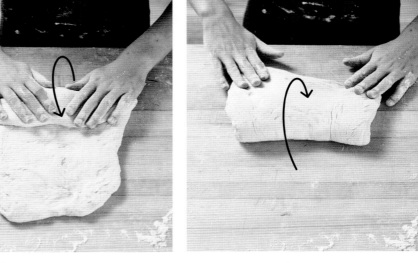

2.

Flatten each piece into a rectangle, and then fold each rectangle into thirds.

3.

Turn the ends under, and place the dough, seam side down, in a greased loaf pan.

4.

Cover with plastic wrap, and let it rise for about 45 minutes, or until doubled in size.

5.

Preheat the oven to 375°F (190°C). Bake for 30 minutes, or until golden brown. Cool in the loaf pan for 10 minutes, and then transfer the loaf to a wire rack. Cool the loaf before eating or storing it.

BRAID AWAY BREAD

Preheat the oven to 375°F (190°C).

KITCHEN CREATIVITY

Egg Wash

A shiny finish gives an elegant look to your homemade bread. Make an egg wash by whisking 1 egg with 2 tablespoons milk or water. Carefully brush it on the unbaked loaves with a pastry brush (be gentle — you don't want the risen bread to sink!). When it comes out of the oven, your bread will have a golden glow.

Makes 1 or 2 loaves

Show off your braiding skills by making this fancy loaf of bread!

Here's What You Need

Easy-Peasy Bread Dough, page 66 (use the full amount for two loaves, or half for one loaf)
Egg wash, (at left)
Fresh herbs, optional

HERE'S WHAT YOU DO

1. If you're making two loaves from a full batch of dough, cut the dough in half. Then divide each half into three equal pieces.

2. Roll each piece into a log 12 to 16 inches long.

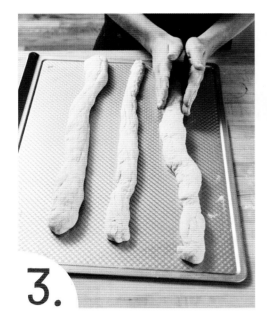

3.

Lay the logs side by side on an oiled baking sheet (or a baking sheet lined with parchment paper).

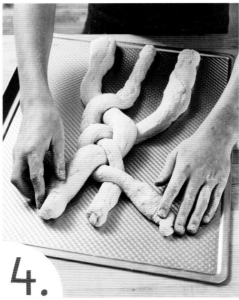

4.

Braid the logs from the center to one end.

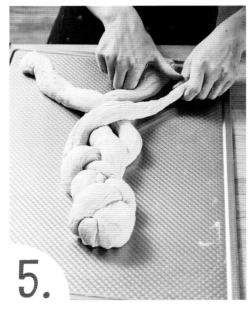

5.

Then braid from the center to the other end.

6.

Pinch the three logs together at each end, and tuck the ends under. Cover with plastic wrap, and let rise for 30 minutes.

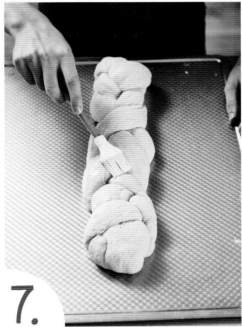

7.

Preheat the oven to 375°F (190°C). Brush the dough with egg wash. Sprinkle with snipped fresh herbs, if you like.

8.

Bake for 25 minutes, or until lightly browned.

Sweet CINNAMON ROLLS

Makes 8–10

Looking for a fancy bread for a holiday breakfast or brunch? These super-tasty cinnamon rolls are sure to be a hit!

Here's What You Need

½ recipe Easy-Peasy Bread Dough, page 66
1–2 tablespoons butter, softened
¼ cup brown sugar
1 tablespoon raisins
1 teaspoon cinnamon
Quick & Easy Glaze (at right)

Preheat the oven to 350°F (180°C).

HERE'S WHAT YOU DO

1. Pat the bread dough into a rectangle about 9 by 13 inches. Spread the softened butter on the dough. Use your (clean) hands!

2. Mix the brown sugar, raisins, and cinnamon in a small bowl. Sprinkle the cinnamon mixture onto the buttered dough.

3. Roll up the dough, jelly-roll style, along the long side. Pinch the edge to seal.

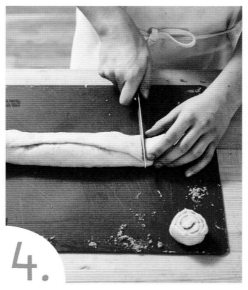

4. Slice the log into 1-inch-thick pieces.

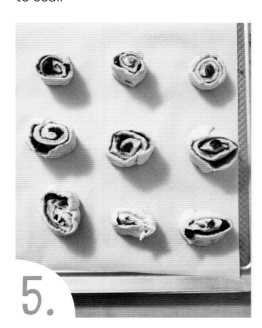

5. Place the rolls on a baking sheet lined with parchment paper. Cover with plastic wrap, and let rise for about 30 minutes.

6. Preheat the oven to 350°F (180°C). Bake for 15 minutes, or until lightly brown. Transfer the cinnamon rolls to a cooling rack. Drizzle on the glaze.

KITCHEN CREATIVITY
Quick & Easy Glaze

Mix up a glaze for your cinnamon rolls! Place 1 cup confectioners' sugar in a bowl, and stir in 2 tablespoons milk, 1 tablespoon at a time, until the mixture is thick but still drips off a spoon. Drizzle it over your cinnamon rolls.

MIX & MATCH
BREAD ART

Play with your food with this fun activity! Make a batch of Easy-Peasy Bread Dough (page 66), and then shape some or all of the bread dough into edible art. Place the dough shapes on a parchment-lined (or oiled) baking sheet and let rise. Preheat the oven to 375°F (190°C). Bake smaller shapes for 15 minutes and bigger ones for up to 30 minutes.

TURTLE

Small Balls for Head, Feet, Tail + Larger Ball Body + Knife Cuts for Shell + Raisin Eyes

OCTOPUS

Oval Ball of Dough + 8 Legs + Raisin Eyes

ON A ROLL

Ball of Dough + Crossmark + Sea Salt

FREAKY FINGERS

Finger Shape Dough + Almond Fingernails + Knife Cuts for Knuckle Markings

SNAIL

Thin Rope Rolled Up + Oblong Body + Raisin Eyes

HAPPY HEDGEHOG

Ball of Dough + Scissor Snips + Raisin Eyes

HEART

Long Thin Snake + Heart Shape

PRETZEL

Long Thin Snake + Twist Twice at Top + Fold Down and Seal

DOUBLE KNOT

Long Thin Snake + Double Knot

SIMPLE TWIST

Long Thin Snake + Twist & Turn

No Need to KNEAD BREAD

Makes 1 loaf

Believe it or not, you can make yummy bread with a crunchy crust without going to a bakery! You need to start this recipe a day before you want to eat your fresh loaf, so plan ahead.

Here's What You Need

- 1½ cups warm water (it should feel like bathwater)
- ¼ teaspoon active dry yeast
- 2 cups all-purpose flour
- 1 cup whole–wheat flour
- 1 tablespoon salt
- 1 tablespoon olive oil

Special Equipment

6- to 8-quart ovenproof pot (cast iron, enamel, Pyrex, or ceramic) with lid

Preheat the oven to 450°F (230°C).

HERE'S WHAT YOU DO

1.
Combine the water and yeast in a large bowl.

2.
Add the flours and salt, and stir until you have a sticky dough.

3. Cover the bowl with plastic wrap. Let it rest for 12 to 18 hours at room temperature.

4. Lightly flour a countertop or cutting board. Scrape the dough onto the counter with a rubber spatula. Sprinkle the sticky dough with a little more flour, and fold it over a few times.

5. Wash and dry the bowl, and then rub the inside with the olive oil. Put the dough back into the bowl, and cover it with plastic wrap. Let it rise for 1½ to 2 hours.

6. Have a grown-up help you put the pot with its lid into the oven, and turn the oven to 450°F (230°C). When the oven is hot, remove the pot (it will be very hot, so be careful).

7. Slip the dough from the bowl into the hot pot. Cover with the lid, return the pot to the oven, and bake for 30 minutes.

8. Remove the lid and bake for another 20 minutes, until the loaf is nice and brown. Have a grown-up help you turn the bread onto a cooling rack. Let it cool for 30 minutes, and then slice it up while it's still nice and warm.

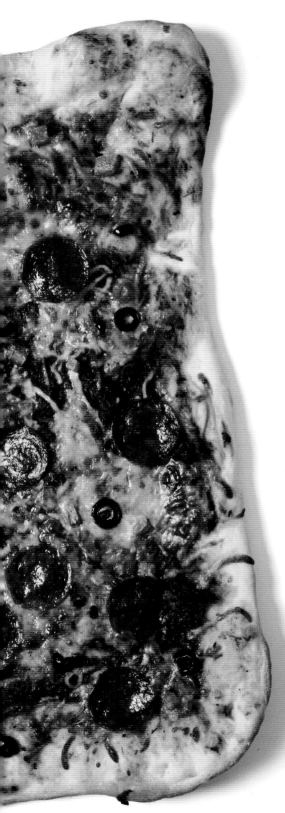

It's a Party!
PIZZA DOUGH

Makes 2 large pizzas

Turn your kitchen into a pizza factory with this easy made-from-scratch dough. It's fun to let friends customize their own pizzas (or part of a pizza) with their favorite toppings.

Here's What You Need

- 1 tablespoon (1 packet) active dry yeast
- 2 teaspoons sugar
- 2½ cups warm water (it should feel like bathwater)
- 6 cups flour
- 2 tablespoons olive oil, plus 1 tablespoon for oiling the bowl

- 2½ teaspoons salt

FOR PIZZA

- 2 cups pizza sauce
- Toppings: olives, green peppers, pepperoni, mushrooms, or whatever you like
- 8 ounces shredded mozzarella cheese

Preheat the oven to 400°F (200°C).

HERE'S WHAT YOU DO

1.

Mix the yeast and sugar in a large bowl. Add the warm water and whisk until dissolved.

2.

Add the flour, 2 tablespoons of the oil, and salt, and stir until you can make a soft ball. Turn the dough onto a lightly floured countertop.

3.

Dust your hands with flour and knead the dough until it is smooth and elastic, about 5 minutes.

4.

Rub the inside of a clean bowl with olive oil. Place the dough in the bowl and turn to coat with oil. Cover with plastic wrap and let it rise for about 30 minutes.

5.

Punch the dough down. Divide it in half, one for each pizza.

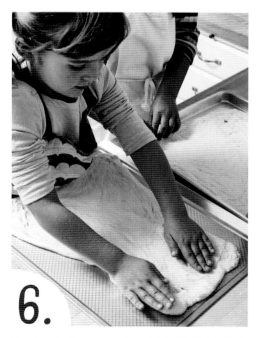

6.

Preheat the oven to 400°F (200°C). Stretch the dough onto lightly oiled baking sheets. If the dough is too hard to flatten out, let it rest for 10 minutes and then try again.

7.

Top with pizza sauce, toppings, and shredded cheese.

8.

Bake for 15 to 20 minutes, or until the cheese is bubbly and the crust is golden brown.

BAKE TREATS

with Friends

Chocolate Chip, Oatmeal, Sugar, Ginger, Coconut, Cinnamon ...

CRISPY GINGERSNAPS, page 94

CHAPTER 5

The COOKIE JAR

Be a smart cookie, and bake up
sweet treats from scratch!

Chocolate Chip COOKIE FACTORY

Makes 2 dozen

Learn how to make this classic cookie so you can pack it in your lunchbox all week long. Be sure to bring extras to share with friends at the lunch table!

Here's What You Need

2¼ cups flour
1 teaspoon baking soda
⅔ teaspoon salt
1 cup (2 sticks) butter, softened
¾ cup sugar
¾ cup packed brown sugar
2 eggs
1 teaspoon vanilla extract
2 cups (16 ounces) chocolate chips

Preheat the oven to 375°F (190°C).

KITCHEN CREATIVITY
Cookie Creativity

* Mix up the size and bake tiny or giant chocolate chip cookies. The baking time will be shorter for smaller cookies and longer for larger ones, so make sure all the cookies on each tray are the same size.

* Bake them on a stick! Slip a popsicle stick into the center before baking.

* Skip the chocolate chips and use white chocolate or butterscotch chips instead.

* Substitute peanut butter chips or toffee bits for half of the chocolate chips to make a candy bar version.

* Bake the dough in a greased 13- by 9- by 2-inch pan for 20 to 25 minutes to make chocolate chip cookie bars!

1.

Stir the flour, baking soda, and salt in a medium bowl.

2.

In a separate large mixing bowl, beat the butter and sugars with an electric mixer.

3.

Beat in the eggs, one at a time. Stir in the vanilla.

4.

Gradually beat in the flour mixture. Stir in the chocolate chips.

5.

Drop the batter by rounded tablespoons onto ungreased baking sheets, using a cookie scoop or spoon. (Line the baking sheets with parchment paper for easier cleanup.)

6.

Bake for 9 to 11 minutes, or until the cookies are just turning golden brown. Let them sit for 2 minutes, and then transfer them to a rack to cool completely.

Awesome OATMEAL COOKIES

Makes about 16 large cookies

Fill your cookie jar with these crispy, chewy, oh-so-delicious cookies. They are made with old-fashioned rolled oats, making them a healthy whole-grain treat!

Here's What You Need

- 1½ cups flour
- 1 teaspoon baking soda
- 1 teaspoon cinnamon
- ½ teaspoon salt
- 1 cup (2 sticks) butter, softened
- ¾ cup sugar
- ¾ cup packed brown sugar
- 1 egg
- 1 teaspoon vanilla extract
- ¾ cup raisins
- 1½ cups old-fashioned rolled oats

Preheat the oven to 375°F (190°C).

HERE'S WHAT YOU DO

1. Stir the flour, baking soda, cinnamon, and salt in a medium bowl.

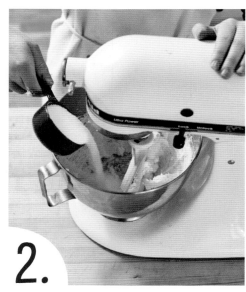

2. In a separate large mixing bowl, cream the butter and sugars with an electric mixer. Beat in the egg. Then mix in the vanilla.

3.

Blend in the flour mixture, and then stir in the raisins and oats.

4.

Drop the batter by tablespoons onto an ungreased baking sheet. Leave at least 2 inches between the cookies because they will spread while baking.

5.

Slightly flatten each cookie with the bottom of a wet glass.

6.

Bake for about 12 minutes, or until the cookies turn a golden brown on the edges. Let cool on the pan for 5 minutes to set, and then transfer to a cooling rack.

KITCHEN CREATIVITY

Super Stir-Ins

Switch up the flavor of your Awesome Oatmeal Cookies by skipping the raisins and adding any of these instead. Try a couple of them together for an extra delicious treat.

* Dried cranberries

* Dried cherries

* Chocolate chips

* White chocolate chips

* Chopped walnuts, almonds, or cashews

Sweet & Simple SUGAR COOKIES

Makes about 2 dozen

This basic recipe can be rolled out and cut into lots of different shapes with cookie cutters. They taste best with cookie frosting and are lots of fun to decorate. Mix up the cookie dough, and then check out Mix & Match Cookie Craft on page 90 for creative ways to shape and design your cookies.

Here's What You Need

- 1 cup (2 sticks) butter, softened
- ¾ cup sugar
- 1 egg
- 1 teaspoon vanilla extract
- 2½ cups flour

Preheat the oven to 375°F (190°C).

Craving Cocoa?

Make chocolate cookies by adding ½ cup unsweetened cocoa powder in step 2.

1. Cream the butter and sugar in a large mixing bowl with an electric mixer. Beat in the egg. Then mix in vanilla.

2. Slowly mix in the flour, and continue mixing until a soft dough forms.

3. Turn the dough out onto the countertop, and pat into two balls. Flatten each into a disk. Wrap in plastic wrap, and chill for at least ½ hour (or up to 4 days).

4. Preheat the oven to 375°F (190°C). Working with one disk at a time, roll out the dough about ⅛ inch thick.

5. Cut out cookies with cookie cutters, and place on an ungreased cookie sheet. Bake for 8 to 10 minutes, or until lightly browned.

6. Cool on the cookie sheet for a few minutes, and then transfer to a cooling rack. Store cooled cookies in a sealed container for up to 1 week.

Sugar Cookie TRICKS

Once you've made the Sweet & Simple Sugar Cookies on the previous page, follow these baker tips and tricks.

USE COLD DOUGH. For best results, cut shapes from cold cookie dough. If the dough is too soft, it will be hard to roll out and will stick to your cutters, and the cookies won't hold their shape. If it starts to feel too soft as you're working, pop it in the fridge for a few minutes.

FREEZE THE DOUGH. Have too much dough? Store it in the fridge for up to 1 week or in the freezer for up to 2 months. When you're ready to bake, just defrost, roll out, and cut into shapes.

SMOOTH ROLLING. Put the dough between two pieces of plastic wrap or waxed paper so it doesn't stick while you roll it out. To flatten the dough evenly, roll the rolling pin back and forth a couple of times, then from side to side. The disk of dough should be not too thick or too thin — about ⅛ inch is just right.

CUTTING SHAPES. Use the sharper side of the cutters to cut out your cookie shapes. Dip the cutters in flour if the dough sticks.

GIVE COOKIE DOUGH ENOUGH SPACE. When you put cookie dough on your cookie sheets, leave at least an inch or two between them. As the cookies bake, they will spread out.

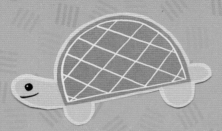

TRACE A TEMPLATE. Instead of cookie cutters, use the templates from the back of the book or cut your own out of cardstock. Place the template on the flattened dough, and trace around it with a paring knife.

SWEETEN WITH A GLAZE! Place 1 cup confectioners' sugar in a bowl, and stir in 2 tablespoons milk, 1 tablespoon at a time, until the mixture is thick but spreadable. Tint with a few drops of food coloring, if you'd like, and frost away! (Tip: For a thicker frosting, mix up a half batch of the Buttercream Frosting on page 126.)

DECORATE! Once you've frosted or glazed your cookies, you can add rainbow or chocolate sprinkles or nonpareils. Or dust frosted cookies with colored sugar.

TOOTHPICK TRICK. For a fun design, spread white glaze over a cookie, then add a few drops of colored glaze and drag a toothpick through the drops, as shown on the tree cookie above.

STRING 'EM UP! To make a hanging ornament out of your cookies, poke a small hole in the dough with a chopstick or toothpick before baking.

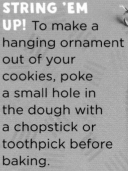

MIX & MATCH
COOKIE CRAFT

Cut your dough into fun shapes with your favorite cookie cutters, or use the templates in the back of the book. Decorate cooled cookies with colored frosting, candy, or other delicious extras. You can also use a pastry bag (see page 130) to draw faces and design your own cookie masterpieces. Here are some ideas to get you started.

TURKEY TROT
Round Cookie + Candy Corn + Chocolate Feet

WHALE
Whale Cookie + Cookie Glaze + Blue Sugar

WISE OWL
Chocolate Owl + Candy Eyes + Gumdrop Nose

FAST FOX
Fox Cookie + Red Frosting + White Nonpareil Tail and Face

OVER THE RAINBOW

Rainbow & Cloud Cookies + Cookie Glaze + Colored Sugar

TINY GINGERBREAD HOUSE
Chocolate Cookie House + White Frosting + Candy

90

SPOOKY GHOST

Cookie Ghost +
Cookie Glaze +
Melted Chocolate
Eyes and Mouth

MINI BURGER

Round Cookie Buns + Red Frosting Ketchup + Mint Patty + Green Coconut Lettuce

RUDOLPH THE REINDEER

Oval Cookie + Pretzel
Antlers + Red Gumdrop Nose

SLOW TURTLE

Turtle Cookie + Green Frosting +
Chocolate Sprinkles

COOKIE STICKS

Cookie Sticks
+ Chocolate
Frosting +
Toppings
(chopped
nuts, coconut,
sprinkles)

SNICKERDOODLES

Makes 2–3 dozen

These buttery cookies are fun to make — you get to roll them in cinnamon sugar before baking them! And they travel well. Treat your teammates to them after a good game!

Here's What You Need

COOKIE DOUGH
- 1⅓ cups flour
- ¾ teaspoon baking powder
- ⅛ teaspoon salt
- ½ cup (1 stick) butter, softened
- ¾ cup sugar
- 1 egg

TOPPING
- ¼ cup sugar
- 2 teaspoons cinnamon

Preheat the oven to 375°F (190°C).

HERE'S WHAT YOU DO

1. Stir the flour, baking powder, and salt in a medium bowl.

2. In a larger bowl, cream the butter and sugar with an electric mixer. Beat in the egg.

3.

Gradually add the flour mixture, mixing well between additions.

4.

Roll the dough into balls about 1½ inches wide.

5.

To make the topping, mix the sugar and cinnamon in a shallow bowl. Roll the balls in the mixture.

6.

Place them on an ungreased baking sheet, about 2 inches apart.

7.

Gently flatten the cookies with the bottom of a glass. Bake for 7 to 10 minutes, or until brown on the edges. Let the cookies sit for 5 minutes on the pan, and then transfer them to a rack to cool completely.

COOKIES FOR A CAUSE

Sarah and Saenger bake gingersnaps, sell them locally for $5 a batch, and send the profits to their favorite charity: Save Our Children.

How did they choose this cause? They realized how lucky they are to have clean water for cooking when there are many people in the world who don't even have clean water for drinking. Save Our Children has a great program that gives families access to clean water. Maybe there's a charity you would like to support this way!

Crispy GINGERSNAPS

Makes about 3 dozen

This cookie recipe is from Sarah and Saenger, two friends who love to bake together and sell their cookies for a cause (read about them at left). These gingersnaps are easy to make — and they stay fresh for a long time, even when shipped to customers through the mail!

Preheat the oven to 350°F (180°C).

Here's What You Need

COOKIE DOUGH
- 2 cups flour
- 2 teaspoons baking soda
- ½ teaspoon salt
- 1 tablespoon ground ginger
- 1 teaspoon cinnamon
- ½ teaspoon ground cloves
- ¾ cup (1½ sticks) butter, softened
- 1 cup sugar
- 1 egg
- ¼ cup molasses
- 1 teaspoon finely grated fresh ginger

TOPPING
- ½ cup sugar
- 2 teaspoons ground ginger

1.

Stir together the flour, baking soda, salt, ground ginger, cinnamon, and cloves in a medium bowl.

2.

In a large bowl, cream the butter and sugar with an electric mixer. Beat in the egg, molasses, and fresh ginger.

3.

Add the flour mixture in two parts, blending at low speed until thoroughly combined.

4.

Line two cookie sheets with parchment paper or grease them. Roll the dough into balls about 2 inches in diameter.

5.

To make the topping, mix the sugar and ground ginger in a shallow bowl. Roll the balls in the topping and place on the cookie sheets, about 2 inches apart.

6.

Bake for 15 to 20 minutes. Let the cookies sit for 5 minutes on the pan, and then transfer them to a rack to cool completely.

COOKIE PACKS

You're one smart cookie if you make your own cookies from scratch! During the school year, pack up your homemade cookies for your lunches. Bake up a batch on the weekend, and then put a few cookies in a reusable container or baggie for each day. Label them with a sticker from the back of the book, and put them in the freezer. You'll enjoy having a sweet treat during your lunch break!

COCONUT MACAROONS

Makes about 14

Craving coconut? Mix up these cookies that are crisp on the outside and soft and sweet on the inside. Look for shredded coconut in the baking section of your grocery store.

Here's What You Need

- ¼ cup flour
- 2 cups shredded coconut
- ⅔ cup sweetened condensed milk
- 1 teaspoon vanilla extract

Preheat the oven to 325°F (170°C).

HERE'S WHAT YOU DO

1. Stir the flour and coconut together in a large mixing bowl.

2. Add the sweetened condensed milk and vanilla and mix well.

3. Line a cookie sheet with parchment paper or grease it. Drop the dough by tablespoons onto the cookie sheet. Make sure the cookies are at least 2 inches apart. Bake for 15 minutes, or until light brown.

4. Immediately remove the cookies from the cookie sheet with a spatula. Place on a cooling rack, and cool for 10 minutes. Drizzle with chocolate if you'd like. (See the drizzling instructions at right.)

KITCHEN CREATIVITY

Chocolate Drizzle

For fancy macaroons, drizzle them with chocolate. Put ¼ cup of chocolate chips in a bowl, and microwave on high for 30 seconds. Stir the chips, and continue microwaving in 10-second bursts until the chips are completely melted. Drizzle the chocolate on top of the cookies with a spoon.

BROWNIE MAGIC

Makes 8–12

Chocolate chips aren't just for cookies. You can use them to make these delicious brownies, too.

Here's What You Need

- ½ cup sugar
- 2 tablespoons butter
- 2 tablespoons water
- 1½ cups (12 ounces) semisweet chocolate chips
- 2 eggs
- ½ teaspoon vanilla extract
- ⅔ cup flour
- ¼ teaspoon baking soda
- ¼ teaspoon salt

Preheat the oven to 325°F (170°C).

HERE'S WHAT YOU DO

1. Grease an 8- by 8-inch square baking pan and set it aside. Stir together the sugar, butter, and water in a medium saucepan over medium heat until it begins to boil.

2. Remove the pan from the heat. Mix in the chocolate chips, stirring until they are all melted. Mix in the eggs and vanilla, and stir vigorously until shiny and smooth.

3. In a separate bowl, stir together the flour, baking soda, and salt. Pour the dry ingredients over the chocolate mixture, and stir them all together until the dry ingredients are just mixed in.

4.

Spread the batter evenly in the greased pan, using a rubber spatula. Bake for 25 to 30 minutes, or until shiny and cracked on top.

5.

Cool the brownies in the pan, and then cut into squares.

KITCHEN CREATIVITY

Brownie Pizza!

Spread the batter in a buttered 12-inch round cake pan, and bake for 25 minutes. Let cool, and then spread with strawberry cream cheese "sauce." Sprinkle on grated coconut "cheese." Top with fresh fruit and mint.

Lots of LEMON SQUARES

Makes 24

For a treat that's both sweet and sour at the same time, try these sunny lemon squares. Here's a favorite recipe that's easy to make.

Preheat the oven to 350°F (180°C).

Here's What You Need

CRUST
- ¾ cup (1½ sticks) butter, at room temperature
- 1½ cups flour
- ⅓ cup confectioners' sugar

FILLING
- 2 or 3 lemons
- 4 eggs
- 1¼ cups sugar
- ⅓ cup flour
- ½ teaspoon vanilla extract

TOPPING
Confectioners' sugar

HERE'S WHAT YOU DO

1.

To make the crust, beat the butter in a large mixing bowl with an electric mixer until fluffy, about 1 minute. Add the flour and confectioners' sugar. Mix until it turns into a soft dough.

2.

Transfer the dough to an ungreased 9- by 13-inch baking pan.

3.

Press the dough into the pan. Bake for 20 minutes, or until the edges start to brown. Take the pan out of the oven and let it cool. Leave the oven turned on.

4.

Zest the lemon using a microplane or the smallest holes on a cheese grater. Cut the lemons in half and squeeze out the juice. Measure ⅓ cup of juice and 1½ tablespoons of zest and set aside.

5.

To make the filling, beat the eggs and sugar together in a large bowl with an electric mixer.

6.

Blend in the flour. Mix in the lemon juice, lemon zest, and vanilla.

7.

Pour the filling over the cooled crust and tilt the pan to spread it evenly.

8.

Bake the bars until the filling is set, about 25 minutes. Cool slightly, then dust lightly with confectioners' sugar using a sifter. Slice into 24 small bars.

SWEET

ENJOY

EASY as PIE!

TEENY TINY APPLE PIES, page 114

CHAPTER 6

SAVE ROOM for PIE!

Roll up your sleeves and roll out the dough — it's time to make pie!

Dig in the Dirt PIE

Makes 6-8 servings

On a hot day, make a mud pie with chocolate ice cream and cookie crumb dirt. Get creative and plant a garden in the dirt. Add any miniature garden supplies you have (like this tiny shovel and watering can!).

Here's What You Need

- 3 pints (1½ quarts) chocolate ice cream
- 1 (11-ounce) package chocolate wafer cookies
- 6 tablespoons butter, melted
- 10–20 fresh mint leaves
- 10–20 fresh blueberries, strawberries, or raspberries

LUCKY LADYBUGS!

Add some critters to your mud pie. To make ladybugs, draw black spots on a red candy with a gourmet writer. You can find gourmet writers at craft and kitchen supply stores. What other bugs can you make?

1. Take the ice cream out of the freezer to soften. Crush the cookies in a ziplock bag with a rolling pin (or pulse in a food processor).

2. Set aside ½ cup of the cookie crumbs. Mix the rest of them with the melted butter in a medium bowl.

3. Press the mixture evenly into the bottom and sides of an ungreased 9 x 9 pan. Place the pan in the freezer for about 10 minutes to set.

4. Spoon the softened ice cream onto the crust, and spread it out with the back of the spoon.

5. Sprinkle the ice cream with the remaining ½ cup cookie crumbs. Top with rows of fresh mint and berries.

6. Freeze overnight. To serve, let the pie stand for a few minutes at room temperature. Slice it with a knife that's been run under hot tap water.

Farmers' Market
FRUIT TARTS

Makes 4

For the world's easiest pie,
start with puff pastry and
fresh fruit. You can buy puff pastry
in the freezer section of your grocery store.
For fruit? Try apples, blueberries, or peaches!

Here's What You Need

1	sheet (½ box) frozen puff pastry, thawed for 40 minutes
2 or 3	apples or peaches, peeled and thinly sliced (or 1½ cups blueberries or raspberries)
¼	cup brown sugar
½	teaspoon cinnamon, optional

**Preheat the oven
to 400°F (200°C).**

HERE'S WHAT YOU DO

1. Roll out the puff pastry on a lightly floured countertop until the dough is about 10 by 12 inches.

2. Cut it into four pieces. Transfer them to a baking sheet lined with parchment paper.

3.

Spread the fruit on top of the squares, leaving about ½ inch of space around the edges.

4.

Stir the brown sugar and cinnamon in a small bowl. Then sprinkle it over the fruit.

5.

Fold up the corners of each square, pinching the sides in place.

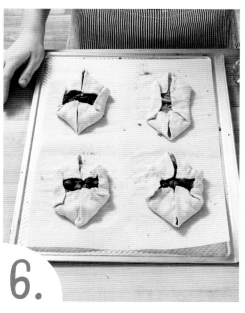

6.

Bake the tarts for 20 to 30 minutes, or until the fruit is soft and the puff pastry is light brown.

LOCAL FLAVOR

For the sweetest, tastiest fruits, buy them in season at a farmers' market or from a pick-your-own place. Look for blueberries, raspberries, apples, peaches, and more, depending on the time of year. If you're craving a simple and delicious treat in the winter, though, you can use frozen fruit (thawed and drained) to make this Farmers' Market Fruit Tart.

Perfect PIECRUST

Makes 2 crusts

The easiest way to mix up a piecrust is in a food processor. The trick is to start with cold butter and ice water and to mix the dough by pressing the pulse button in short bursts. Don't mix it too much or your crust may turn out chewy instead of flaky and tender.

Here's What You Need

- 3 cups flour
- 2 tablespoons sugar
- ¼ teaspoon salt
- 1 cup (2 sticks) cold butter, cut into small pieces
- 8–10 tablespoons ice water

Tip: Don't have a food processor? You can mix the ingredients together in a large bowl with a pastry cutter or even two forks. It's a little harder to get the mixture to look sandy, so use your muscles!

HERE'S WHAT YOU DO

1.
Place the flour, sugar, and salt in the bowl of a food processor. Pulse once or twice to mix it up. Add the butter, and mix in short pulses until it looks sandy.

2.
Sprinkle with the ice water, and process in pulses until the dough starts to come together. It should still be slightly crumbly.

3.
Divide the dough in half, and place on sheets of plastic wrap. Pat each half into a ball, gathering up all the crumbs.

4.

Flatten each ball into a thick disk. Wrap the disks in plastic. Refrigerate for at least 20 minutes (or up to 2 days).

5.

Before using the dough, let it soften slightly at room temperature. Roll it out between two pieces of plastic wrap, following the directions for the recipe you are using it for.

HOW TO LINE A PIE PAN

1 Once your crust is rolled out, carefully fold it into quarters.

2 Transfer it to a pie pan with the corner point in the center, and then unfold.

3 Press the crust gently into the pie pan.

4 Trim the edges with a knife.

5 Crimp the edges into a pattern (see page 110 for ideas). Don't worry about getting the crust to look perfect. Even imperfect pies taste terrific!

MIX & MATCH
PIECRUST SHAPES

Once you've made your basic piecrust, you can get creative with shaping and crimping it. Each pie will look a little different, but they will all taste the same — delicious! Begin by lining a pie pan with the crust (see How to Line a Pie pan on page 109). Then follow one of the recipes in this chapter for the filling and baking. Happy pie making!

LATTICE

Use a pastry wheel or knife to cut the dough into strips. Weave them over the pie.

SPOON CRIMPED

Decorate the crust edge by pressing with the rounded end of a spoon.

SLAB PIE

Instead of using a pie pan, use a small square sheet pan.

PIE ORNAMENTS

Cut out small stars and other shapes to bake on top of the pie.

FORK CRIMPED

Decorate the crust edge by pressing with the tines of a fork.

PIE PATTERN

Use a cookie cutter to cut out shapes in the top crust.

FINGER CRIMPED

Crimp your crust by pressing a finger into the dough as you pinch it with your other hand.

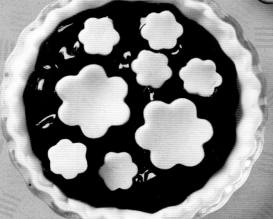

111

My First
BLUEBERRY
PIE

Makes 8–10 servings

If you're looking for an easy first pie, try this one. You don't need to do any slicing or dicing — just pile plump, ripe berries into a piecrust and bake it up. Top with a scoop of vanilla ice cream.

Here's What You Need

- 5 cups fresh blueberries
- ⅔ cup sugar
- ¼ cup flour
- 1 tablespoon lemon juice
- 2 unbaked piecrusts (page 108)
- 2 tablespoons butter, cut into chunks

Preheat the oven to 400°F (200°C).

HERE'S WHAT YOU DO

1.
Stir the blueberries with the sugar, flour, and lemon juice in a large bowl.

2.
Roll out half of the piecrust dough between two pieces of plastic wrap to ⅛-inch thickness. Line the bottom of an ungreased 9-inch pie pan with the rolled dough.

3.

Fill the pie shell with the blueberry mixture. Dot the butter chunks across the top.

4.

Roll out the second ball of dough. Cut it into ½-inch-wide strips with a pastry wheel or knife. Place half the strips on top of the pie, leaving about 1 inch between each strip.

5.

Weave the remaining strips over and under to make a lattice top. Trim off any overhanging strips with a knife.

6.

Press the tines of a fork around the edges. Bake for 40 minutes, or until the filling bubbles and the crust turns golden brown.

KITCHEN CREATIVITY

Fruit Pie Flavors

Switch up your blueberry pie, and try one of these fruits instead.

APPLE PIE
- 5 cups apple slices
- ½ cup sugar
- 1 tablespoon flour
  Juice of half a lemon
- ½ teaspoon cinnamon
- ¼ teaspoon nutmeg
- 1 tablespoon butter, cut into chunks

Bake for 40 minutes at 400°F (200°C).

STRAWBERRY / RHUBARB
- 4 cups sliced strawberries
- 2 cups diced rhubarb
- ¾ cup sugar
- ¼ cup flour
- 1 tablespoon butter, cut into chunks

Bake for 45 minutes at 400°F (200°C).

SAVE ROOM FOR PIE!

Teeny Tiny
APPLE PIES

Makes 12

These tiny treats will fit in the palm of your hand. These are made with apples, but you can use raspberries or blueberries instead.

Here's What You Need

1. apple, peeled, cored, and chopped (or 1 cup berries)
2. tablespoons sugar
1. teaspoon cinnamon
2. teaspoons orange juice
2. unbaked piecrusts (see page 108)
1. tablespoon butter
1. egg
1. tablespoon milk

Preheat the oven to 375°F (190°C).

HERE'S WHAT YOU DO

1. Mix the chopped apple, sugar, cinnamon, and juice in a bowl. Set it aside for about 10 minutes to get nice and juicy.

2. Roll out the piecrust between two pieces of plastic wrap.

3.

Cut out twelve 2½-inch circles with a round cookie cutter or rim of a glass. Press each one into a cup of a mini muffin pan. You don't need to grease the cups.

4.

Add 1 rounded tablespoon of filling to each cup. Dot with a tiny piece of the butter.

5.

Gather the dough scraps and roll them out. Use tiny cookie cutters to make decorative shapes or cut thin strips for lattice toppings.

6.

Add a top crust with slits, a cut-out shape, or a lattice top. Crimp the edges together with a fork or your fingers.

7.

Beat the egg with the milk in a small bowl. Brush the mini pies with the egg mixture. Bake for 15 to 17 minutes, or until the crusts are golden-brown.

8.

Let the pies cool for just a few minutes in the pan, and then carefully remove each one by running a sharp knife around the edges and popping it out of the pan.

PEACHY KEEN CRUMBLE

Makes 6–8 servings

Pick your own peaches, and mix up this yummy dessert!

Preheat the oven to 375°F (190°C).

Here's What You Need

- 6 ripe peaches
- 1½ cups rolled oats
- ⅔ cup brown sugar
- 3 tablespoons flour
- 1 tablespoon cinnamon
- ½ cup (1 stick) butter, softened

HERE'S WHAT YOU DO

1. Peel and slice the peaches. Spread the slices evenly in an ungreased 8- or 9-inch square pan.

2. Stir together the oats, brown sugar, flour, and cinnamon in a medium bowl.

116

3.

Add the softened butter, and mix with a fork or pastry cutter until crumbly. Or mix it up with your (clean!) hands.

4.

Crumble the topping evenly over the fruit.

5.

Bake for 40 to 45 minutes, or until the topping is light brown and the juices start to bubble. Spoon it into a bowl and enjoy warm.

GO BANANAS CREAM PIE

Makes 8–10 servings

If you love vanilla pudding and bananas, this creamy-dreamy pie is sure to become a favorite.

Here's What You Need

CRUST

- 12 graham crackers
- 6 tablespoons butter, melted

FILLING

- ¾ cup sugar
- ⅓ cup cornstarch
- ⅛ teaspoon salt
- 3 cups milk
- 3 egg yolks
- 2 teaspoons vanilla extract
- 2–3 bananas
  Whipped cream (see instructions at right)

HERE'S WHAT YOU DO

1. To make the crust, crush the graham crackers in a food processor or in a plastic bag with a rolling pin. Pour the crumbs into a bowl, add the melted butter, and stir it up.

2. Press the crust into the bottom and sides of a 9-inch pie plate. Place in the freezer for 10 minutes to set.

3. To make the filling, whisk the sugar, cornstarch, and salt in a medium saucepan. Then whisk in the milk and the egg yolks.

4. Heat the milk mixture over medium heat, stirring until it thickens and bubbles, about 5 minutes. Continue cooking and stirring until it coats your spoon, another minute or two. Turn off the heat. Stir in the vanilla.

5. Pour the hot filling into the piecrust. Cover with plastic wrap, and refrigerate for several hours or overnight.

6. Remove the plastic wrap. Slice the bananas and arrange them evenly over the pudding.

7. Spread a thick layer of fresh whipped cream over the pie. Add extra banana slices on top of the pie. Slice it up and serve!

Whipped Cream

The best topping for pies and other desserts is a big dollop of whipped cream. Here's how to mix it up.

HERE'S WHAT YOU NEED

- 1 pint cold heavy or whipping cream
- 2–3 tablespoons confectioners' (or regular) sugar
- 2 teaspoons vanilla extract

HERE'S WHAT YOU DO

1. Pour the cold cream into a mixing bowl. Start beating it with an electric mixer.

2. When the cream starts to thicken, stop mixing and add the sugar and vanilla.

3. Keep whipping! Watch for soft peaks to form — or whip until stiffer peaks form. But be careful: too much mixing could turn your cream into butter!

cake time

YIPPPEE!

BEAT IT!

AFTER-SCHOOL APPLE CAKE, page 138

CHAPTER 7

CAKE & CUPCAKE FACTORY

Baking is a piece of cake with the easy and delicious recipes in this chapter!

COCOA
CAKE-IN-A-MUG

Makes 1 serving

This easy cake-in-a-mug is a quick fix for a chocolate craving. It makes enough for just one person — and because you microwave it, it's ready to eat in 5 minutes!

Here's What You Need

- 1 tablespoon butter
- 1 egg
- ¼ cup sugar
- 3 tablespoons unsweetened cocoa powder
- Confectioners' sugar (for garnish)

HERE'S WHAT YOU DO

1. Microwave the butter in a mug for 10 to 20 seconds, until melted. Crack the egg into a separate bowl and whisk it slightly. Pour it over the butter, and whisk away.

2. Beat in the sugar and cocoa powder.

3. Cook in the microwave on high for 1 minute, or until a toothpick inserted in the center comes out clean. Sift a little confectioners' sugar on top for a garnish. Dig in with a spoon.

Sprinkle on Sugar Decorations

USE THE STENCILS IN THE BACK OF THE BOOK to create fancy patterns on your cupcakes and cookies with confectioners' sugar. First, put ½ to 1 cup of confectioners' sugar in a sifter or small fine-mesh strainer. Lay a stencil lightly on the surface of the baked good and gently shake or tap the container over it, making sure to cover the whole design. Very carefully lift the stencil straight up and away from the surface.

Stenciling with confectioners' sugar is messy — put the cupcakes or cookies on a baking sheet or plate!

Don't use the handle of the sifter because too much sugar might come out at once.

On vanilla cookies or cupcakes, use granulated sugar tinted with a few drops of food coloring. Brush the surface lightly with juice first so the sugar sticks.

Very Vanilla BIRTHDAY CAKE

Makes 8–10 servings

This classic yellow cake is sweet and buttery. Follow the basic batter recipe, and then bake it in any of the pans listed below.

Here's What You Need

- 1 cup (2 sticks) butter, at room temperature
- 2 cups sugar
- 4 eggs
- 1 tablespoon vanilla extract
- 3 cups flour
- 1 tablespoon baking powder
- ¼ teaspoon salt
- 1⅓ cups buttermilk

BAKING TIMES

Two 8- or 9-inch round or square pans

45 minutes

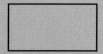
One 13- by 9- by 2-inch pan

45 minutes

Two 12-cup muffin pans

20 minutes

Preheat the oven to 350°F (180°C).

1. Butter and lightly flour the cake pan(s) of your choice. We used two 8-inch rounds.

2. Beat the butter and sugar in a large bowl using an electric mixer until light and fluffy, about 5 minutes.

3. Beat in the eggs, one at a time, until combined. Beat in the vanilla.

4. In a separate bowl, whisk the flour, baking powder, and salt. With the mixer on low, add half of the flour mixture to the butter mixture, and beat until just combined.

5. Beat in half of the buttermilk. Add the remaining flour mixture and buttermilk separately, beating after each addition until just combined. Scrape down the bowl as needed.

6. Pour the batter into the prepared pan(s). Bake according to the times listed at left, or until a toothpick inserted in the center comes out clean.

Flavored Frostings

CHOCOLATE ICING.
Substitute 1 cup of unsweetened cocoa powder for an equal amount of confectioners' sugar.

CREAM CHEESE FROSTING.
Substitute 4 to 6 ounces of softened cream cheese for the same amount of butter.

BUTTERCREAM FROSTING

Makes 3 cups

This sweet, smooth frosting goes with all kinds of cakes and cupcakes. Tint the whole batch a favorite color, or color just a portion of it to pipe on decorative swirls and designs.

Here's What You Need

- 1 cup (2 sticks) butter, at room temperature
- 3¾ cups confectioners' sugar
- 1 teaspoon vanilla extract
- 3–4 tablespoons milk

HERE'S WHAT YOU DO

1.

Beat the butter in a large bowl with an electric mixer until it's nice and creamy.

2.

Slowly add the confectioners' sugar, mixing at low speed.

3.

Add the vanilla and 2 tablespoons of the milk, and mix at low speed.

4.

Mix until the frosting is smooth and creamy. If it's too thick, you can add more milk a bit at a time to make it more spreadable.

BAKE UP A BIRTHDAY PARTY!

Looking for a fun theme for your next birthday party? Host a baking party! Send out invitations on recipe cards. Serve make-your-own pizzas from scratch (see page 78). Check out the decorating tips on page 134 and put out lots of fun materials so your guests can decorate their own cupcakes. For favors, send guests home with wooden spoons and aprons, decorated at the party. Happy birthday!

FROSTING for Beginners

1. START WITH A COMPLETELY COOLED CAKE. If you frost the cake while it's still warm, the butter in your icing will melt! You can freeze the cake before you frost it to make it super easy to spread the frosting.

2. IF THE CAKE IS TOO CRUMBLY, MAKE A CRUMB COAT FIRST. To do this, spread a thin layer of frosting on the cake to seal in the crumbs. Then refrigerate or freeze the cake for 15 minutes. Now you can frost the whole cake without making a big mess!

3. FROST THE TOP OF THE CAKE FIRST, beginning with a pile of frosting in the center and spreading it out to the sides. Next, frost the sides of the cake, working from the top to the bottom.

4. IF THE SPREADER BECOMES TOO GOOEY, dip it in a glass of warm water to clean it off for easier spreading.

Use a straight-edged metal spatula like this one for a smoothly frosted cake.

HOW TO COLOR FROSTING

1 Divide the frosting into small bowls, one for each color. Squirt a few drops of food coloring into each bowl. Mix it all up.

2 For vibrant colored frosting, use paste food colors. Add dabs of the paste to your frosting with a toothpick — a little paste goes a long way!

3 For all-natural colored frosting, make dye out of fresh raspberries. Push the berries through a strainer so the juice runs into the icing. Stir it up. Add more juice until the color is just right.

CAKE DECORATING BASICS

With a pastry bag, a few decorating tips, and buttercream frosting, you can create all kinds of playful designs on your cakes and cupcakes. Start with a pastry kit that has decorator tips (we use a Wilton set). You can tell the decorator tips apart by their names and numbers.

PASTRY BAG TIPS

Read your pastry kit directions to assemble the pastry bag.

- For one like this, the first step is to slip the plastic coupler inside the bag. Slide the decorator tip over the coupler outside the bag. Twist the ring over the tip and lock the tip in place.

- Set the bag into a tall drinking glass, tucking the ends over the sides of the glass.

- Fill the bag with frosting, tamping it right down into the end of the bag to get rid of air bubbles.

- Test your designs on waxed paper before you decorate your cakes and cupcakes.

STAR TIP

Use this tip to make a festive border around your cake. Or make mini flowers or a swirled design on a cupcake.

LEAF TIP

Create basic or ruffled leaves with this tip. Hold the bag at a 45-degree angle so that the tip opening is horizontal, squeeze out frosting, and slowly pull up the tip when you have the desired leaf length.

ROUND TIP

You can make polka dot borders with this tip, draw thick letters and numbers, or create a swirl on top of a cupcake.

RIBBON TIP

This narrow tip makes flat ribbon lines on cupcake (the mummy on page 135 was made with this tip!).

WRITING TIP

Use this tiny round tip for writing messages, drawing or outlining shapes, and making dots.

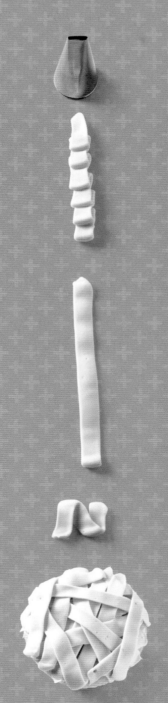

One-Bowl CHOCOLATE CUPCAKES

Makes 24

If you're in the mood for chocolate cupcakes, but you're out of milk, eggs, and butter, here's a quick and easy vegan recipe that will do the trick. Or you can use the same batter to make an equally quick and easy cake!

Here's What You Need

2 cups sugar
3 cups flour
2 teaspoons baking soda
1 teaspoon salt
¾ cup unsweetened cocoa powder
2 cups water
¾ cup vegetable or olive oil
2 tablespoons white vinegar
2 teaspoons vanilla extract

Preheat the oven to 350°F (180°C).

BAKING TIMES

Two 8- or 9-inch round or square pans

30 minutes

One 13- by 9- by 2-inch pan

40 minutes

Two 12-cup muffin pans

25 minutes

1.

Line two 12-cup muffin pans with paper liners. If you're making a cake, grease the pan.

2.

Stir the sugar, flour, baking soda, salt, and cocoa powder in a large bowl.

3.

Add the water, vegetable oil, vinegar, and vanilla. Mix it up with a spoon until nice and smooth.

4.

Pour the batter into the muffin pans until they are two-thirds full. Bake for 25 minutes (longer for a cake), or until a toothpick inserted in the center comes out clean.

I LOVE Chocolate ♥ ♥ ♥

MIX & MATCH

CUPCAKE DECORATING PARTY

Bake cupcakes, set out colored frosting and sprinkles, and invite friends and family to roll up their sleeves and design edible masterpieces. At the end of the party, be sure to arrange the cupcakes on a table so everyone can ooh and aah. Here are some sweet ideas to get you started:

CUB CAKE

Mini Peppermint Patty Paw + Chocolate Chip Toes + White Cupcake + Shredded Coconut

BRIGHT BALLOONS

Bright Colored Cupcakes + Shoestring Licorice

SPOOKY SWEETS

White Frosting
Mummy Stripes
+ Candy Eyes

SPRING BUTTERFLY

Mini Pretzel Wings + M&M
Head + Gummy Worm
Body + Licorice Antennae

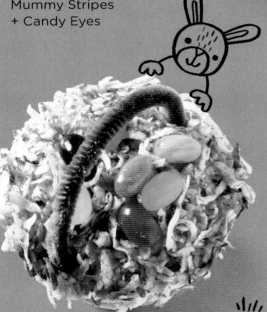

EASTER BASKET

Pipe Cleaner + Jelly Beans
+ Green Coconut Grass

FRUIT FLOWERS

Almond Petals
+ Berry Flower
Center

Say "CHEESE!" CAKE

Makes 8–10 servings

This creamy cheesecake is made with a graham cracker crust and a cream cheese filling. Top it with fresh berry sauce for extra flavor.

Preheat the oven to 350°F (180°C).

Here's What You Need

CRUST
- 10 graham crackers
- 5 tablespoons butter, melted

FILLING
- 3 (8-ounce) packages cream cheese, softened
- 1 cup sugar
- 2 tablespoons flour
- 4 eggs
- 3 tablespoons heavy cream
- ½ teaspoon vanilla extract
- 1 teaspoon grated lemon or orange zest, optional

STRAWBERRY SAUCE
- 1 pint strawberries, stemmed
- 1 tablespoon sugar
- 2 tablespoons lemon juice

Special Equipment
8- or 9-inch springform pan

HERE'S WHAT YOU DO

1. To make the crust, crush the graham crackers in a food processor or in a plastic bag with a rolling pin. Add the melted butter, and stir to combine.

2. Press the crust into the bottom and sides of an 8- or 9-inch springform pan. Place in the freezer for 10 minutes to set.

3.

Whip the cream cheese in a bowl with an electric mixer until fluffy. Add the sugar, flour, eggs, cream, vanilla, and lemon zest, and blend thoroughly.

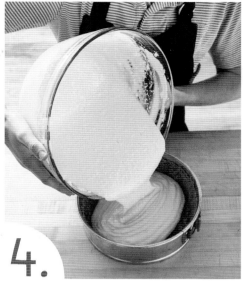

4.

Pour the filling over the crust.

5.

Bake for 1 hour, or until the center is set and no longer jiggly. Cool completely (or refrigerate overnight).

6.

Make a fresh berry sauce by blending the strawberries with the sugar and lemon juice. Drizzle it over slices of cheesecake.

After-School APPLE CAKE

Makes 15–18 servings

When apples are in season, bake up this favorite fall dessert. Enjoy it after school or dinner and pack extras in your lunchbox for a wholesome school sweet.

Here's What You Need

6	apples	1	tablespoon
2	teaspoons cinnamon		baking powder
¾	cup vegetable oil	1½	cups all-purpose flour
4	eggs	½	cup whole-wheat
1¼	cups sugar		flour

Preheat the oven to 350°F (180°C).

1.

Have a grown-up help you peel, core, and thinly slice the apples. Place them in a large bowl and sprinkle with the cinnamon.

2.

In another large bowl, blend the oil, eggs, and sugar with a whisk.

3.

Add the baking powder and flours, and mix well.

4.

Pour the batter over the apples, gently stirring until the apples are just coated.

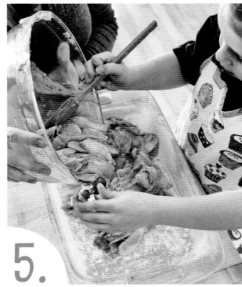

5.

Grease and flour a 13- by 9- by 2-inch pan. Scrape the batter into the pan with a spatula, and spread it into an even layer.

6.

Bake for 35 to 45 minutes, or until a toothpick inserted in the center comes out clean. Cool the cake in the pan before cutting it into small squares.

Mini STRAWBERRY SHORTCAKES

Makes 6

These bite-size treats are a fun, fresh dessert to make when strawberry season starts.

Here's What You Need

- 2 pints fresh strawberries, sliced (about 5 cups)
- 5 tablespoons sugar
- 1¾ cups flour
- ½ teaspoon salt
- 1 tablespoon baking powder
- 4 tablespoons butter
- ½ cup milk
  Whipped cream, for topping (page 119)
  Mini chocolate chips (optional)

Preheat the oven to 350°F (180°C).

HERE'S WHAT YOU DO

1. Place the sliced strawberries in a large bowl, and sprinkle with 2 tablespoons of the sugar. Stir well. Cover, and let the berries sit for at least 1 hour, or until some juice forms in the bottom of the bowl.

2. Preheat the oven to 350°F (180°C). Mix the remaining 3 tablespoons sugar with the flour, salt, baking powder, and butter in a large bowl with a pastry cutter until the mixture looks sandy.

3. Add the milk, and mix to form a soft dough.

4. Turn the dough out onto a lightly floured surface, and roll to ¼-inch thickness.

5. Cut out the shortcakes with a small, round cookie cutter or the top of a spice jar. Place the rounds on an ungreased cookie sheet, and bake for 8 to 10 minutes.

6. When you're ready to serve, slice the shortcakes in half, and place the bottoms on plates. Spoon a few strawberries over each shortcake, and add a dollop of whipped cream.

7. Place the tops of the shortcakes on the whipped cream, followed by another layer of whipped cream and a few more strawberries. Enjoy as is, or garnish with mini chocolate chips!

INDEX

BONUS FEATURES!

DESIGN STENCILS.
Sift confectioners sugar over these cool stencils to make a fancy pattern on your cakes and cookies.

COOKIE CUTTER TEMPLATES.
Lay the shape on your rolled-out dough and carefully cut around the outline with a knife to make all kinds of crazy cookies!

STICKERS & LABELS.
Some are meant to be folded onto a toothpick and used to decorate cupcakes, muffins, pies — or whatever you want! Some are labels for giving yummy baked goods as gifts, but most of them are just for fun.

GIFT TAGS.
Everyone loves a homemade treat. Bake up some batches of goodies for teachers, relatives, and friends.

BAKE SALE SIGNS.
A bake sale is a sure-fire fundraiser!

THIS BAKING KIT BELONGS to

THIS BAKING KIT BELONGS TO:

LICK THE BOWL

BEAT IT!

Made for You by:

Made for You by:

I LOVE Chocolate

I WANT CAKE

BAKED WITH LOVE

FOR:

BAKED WITH LOVE

FOR:

SMART COOKIE

SAVE ROOM FOR PIE!

YUMMY TREATS FOR YOU

TO:
FROM:

YUMMY TREATS FOR YOU

TO:
FROM:

BROWNIE POINTS!

SUGAR AND SPICE

SNACK ATTACK

Peachy Keen!